COACHING
WHOLE SCHOOL CHANGE

COACHING
WHOLE SCHOOL CHANGE

Lessons in Practice from a
Small High School

David Allen

with
Suzanne Wichterle Ort, Alexis Constantini,
Jennie Reist, and Joseph Schmidt

Foreword by THOMAS SOBOL
Afterword by SYLVIA RABINER

Teachers College
Columbia University
New York and London

Published by Teachers College Press, 1234 Amsterdam Avenue, New York, NY 10027

Library of Congress Cataloging-in-Publication Data

Allen, David, 1961–
  Coaching whole school change : lessons in practice from a small high school / David Allen with Suzanne Wichterle Ort . . . [et al.] ; foreword by Thomas Sobol ; afterword by Sylvia Rabiner.
      p. cm.
  Includes bibliographical references.
  ISBN 978-0-8077-4902-9 (pbk. : alk. paper)
  1. Assistant school principals—United States. 2. High schools—United States—Administration—Case studies. 3. Group facilitation. I. Ort, Suzanne Wichterle. II. Title.
  LB2831.92.A45 2008
  372.24′2—dc22

                                                                                          2008022147

ISBN 978-0-8077-4902-9 (paperback)

Printed on acid-free paper

Manufactured in the United States of America

15 14 13 12 11 10 09 08   8 7 6 5 4 3 2 1

Contents

Foreword

They used to come by other names. Generically, they were called "supervisors," "assistant principals," "team leaders," or, if the program involved secondary schools, "department heads." Looking from the top down, school administrators agreed that some kind of position, somewhere on the totem pole between teacher and principals, was needed to check that the approved curriculum was being taught and the approved kind of teaching was being followed. Looking from the bottom up, teachers saw at worst threats and at best ineffectiveness; the embarrassed and embarrassing trivia of those who don't "get it." In most schools the term "supervisor" evoked a mildly amusing stereotype, an authoritarian type armed with a no-nonsense clipboard and the eyes of a hawk, eager to pounce on a misaligned bulletin board or an unopened window. Not a bad idea, that opening of the window, but one not likely by itself to improve teaching and learning.

No more. Exit the traditional supervisors and enter the newly formed ranks of "coaches." Steeped in practical knowledge and eager to share it with others, "coaches" work with individual and small groups of teachers to help them improve classroom practice. Their work builds on cherished (albeit frequently challenged) tenets of progressive theory. Learning is a constructive process: We learn from what we have learned, as well as from what we are learning. Knowledge is gained through action, including the act of reflection. Quality and creativity—not compliance—are the goals. Learning is a social activity, at least most of the time.

I find it amusing that the business community, which has long criticized such "soft and muddle-headed notions," now emerges as the champion of coaching and all its actions and beliefs. We have business coaching, leadership coaching, legal coaching, medical coaching, and so on. What's in a name? Does "coaching" evoke a positive, familiar activity in American life, whereas, say, "professional development specialist" does not? A few years ago the people who do this work would have been called additions to the education bureaucracy. Now they are at the forefront of education reform. Ironically, the "coaching" they do in the schools is seen as an adaptation of sound business practice, when the truth is the other way around.

No matter. For centuries teachers have learned to plant seeds and let students take the credit when they grow. In this book, the authors' goal is to describe in sensitive, perceptive detail how coaching developed in one school over a period of 5 years. However, as the authors state, "The book is not intended as a comprehensive account of how Park East High School developed or a catalog of all of the coaching actions that have taken place there in the 5 years we have been involved with the school. Instead, we focus on specific moments from the life of the school during that period to illuminate the nature of coaching practice."

And so they do. The heart of this book is the detailed descriptions of coaching relationships as they were worked out over the years. The authors eschew academic abstraction and deal with what people see and say and feel—with the relationships and reality of classroom life. And because they are gifted teachers themselves, we get an extra treat—a vivid portrait of good teaching and what it looks like when teachers and students are helped to think, question, and imagine "on their own." Consider the following excerpt by Alexis, one of the contributors to this book, who is being coached.

> In trying to teach the water cycle to a group of uninterested ninth graders I veered off topic and tried to grasp their attention by talking about the waste water cycle. As I described what happens to their goldfish when it gets flushed down the toilet, a student spoke up and asked if we could watch a movie about what happens to water. I mistakenly took that to mean a movie on the water cycle and soon after I showed them a film about evaporation, cloud formation, and precipitation. When the film was over, she was angry because she meant she wanted to see something about "our water." This is when it dawned on me that she wanted to see what happened to sewage.
>
> At our next meeting, Suzy and I came up with two questions for the students to investigate: "What's better to drink: bottled water or Park East school water?" and "Where in the school is the best water?" We decided these questions would have a direct impact on the students' lives considering they love to complain about the water fountains and how that water is "gross." Since we would be conducting the experiment during the Human Impact section of the curriculum these guiding questions would allow for some real world experience to drive their learning experience.

I allowed time for developing concepts, including pollution and the role of humans on the environment. We thought about what the students might need to have reinforced before we started the experiment, specifically which data to collect, how to collect it, and the importance of more than one trial. We also discussed how to tie into the experiment a trip to the sewage treatment plant and how to relate the students' investigations to what they would see when going to the plant.

The students would be broken into four groups and they would first develop two separate hypotheses based on the two guiding questions and then perform tests which measured the pH, alkalinity, hardness, sulfite, iron, and chloride content of their water. Each day we went to the lab, each group would do several trials for two of the different tests. We also decided that each group would be testing a different floor of the school and different type of bottled water and then comparing it to their classmates' data before drawing any conclusions. I would need to explain the pH scale to the students and briefly discuss what the presence of each of the chemicals would mean for the purity of their water.

Soft? Muddle-headed? Or proof that all of us, properly coached, can learn?

Some truth-in-lending provision prompts me to disclose the fact that Suzy Ort and David Allen were once students in a course I taught. I suppose that protocol forbids me from expressing the respect and admiration I feel for these young people. Suffice it to say that they were my coaches then, and are now, and evermore shall be.

Thomas Sobol
Christian A. Johnson Professor, Emeritus
Teachers College, Columbia University

Acknowledgments

The authors would like to thank Gerry House, Jackie Ancess, Sylvia Rabiner, Phyllis Tashlik, Marc Siciliano, and Sandy Abrams for their insight and support, as well as all the ISA coaches for the opportunity to learn with and from them. We also thank Alan Dichter, Anthony Conelli, Tom Sobol, and Joseph McDonald for their encouragement and participation in our project.

We give our special thanks to Park East High School principals Nick Mazzarella and Kevin McCarthy for opening up their school to our inquiry. We are grateful to the inspiring faculty (current and former) at Park East, who worked with us to make this book possible: John Giambalvo, Drew Allsopp, Marcia Edmonds, Clancy McKenna, Liz Lauben, Lisa Purcell, Peter Polak, Chris Pace, Jeannette MacNish, Jackie Mittman, Brianne Tafuro, Ed Poli, David Arthur, Carrie Worthington, John Ambrose, Lauren Brady, Shernell Thomas, Lynelle Rennis, Dyanand Sugrim, Diedre Downing, Nicole Palmiotto, Paul Feinberg, and Yessenia Briceno.

Our individual acknowledgments follow. *Suzy:* "I would like to thank my family—Hynek, Klara, and Johan—for listening to endless Park East stories; my mother-in-law, Hana, for providing babysitting at critical moments; and my brother, Tommy, and his wife, Mani, for their academic eyes and for always suggesting good books to read." *Alexis:* "To mom, Patti, and step-father, Chuck, for always encouraging me to try new things. And to those very special people, whom I can always count on in traffic to listen to my Park East stories, and let me just talk." *Joe:* "To Claudia and Gabe for their support and understanding. To my parents, Peter and Randi, who taught me what it means to be a teacher." *Jennie*: "I would like to thank my parents and sisters, who gave me much support during my 2 years teaching at Park East." *David*: "Thanks to Tina Blythe for her perceptive reading of the manuscript; Ruth Vinz and Tom Hatch for their patient, insightful advising; all my NCREST colleagues and friends; and Dan, Robyn, Finnian, and Lucy for many many reviving and regaling meals."

Finally, we all would like to recognize with a big "shout out" to the students at Park East—who are the reason why.

CHAPTER 1

Introduction:
Coaching as a Professional Practice

In the physical education office, the school-change coach is speaking with a new teacher from Slovakia. She is helping him find a way to deal with a frustrating situation: a very large gym class, students wandering in late and socializing rather than taking part in the activities he is trying to lead. She suggests identifying just a small number of students willing to participate in soccer drills: "Identify a group of students willing to do the activities, demonstrate with them, and have them help to pull the others in."

As the full-faculty professional development session gets under way during first period in the school library, Ed, a former teacher returning to work part-time to support the new special education teachers, sits down next to the coach. Quickly she introduces him to Brianne, a second-year social studies teacher, telling him, "Brianne does great poster projects with her students." The coach suggests one of the things he could do in his emerging job description is to work with her on developing the student projects by using PowerPoint, something he had done while teaching at the school.

In between classes, the coach runs into one of the teachers she meets with regularly in the hallway. She flips open her notebook and pulls off a Post-it note. "Joe, I had a few things I wanted to talk to you about . . . "

The three very brief moments above suggest just a few of the myriad activities a school coach might engage in during a typical day in the school. Any coach could offer countless others from their own experience—from those that occur repeatedly, such as meeting with new and developing teachers, to those that come up unexpectedly, such as helping to figure out what to do when a phys ed class gets moved to the library just before the bell rings and the teacher does not have time to prepare a classroom-based lesson. As coaching becomes more common in our schools, it will be increasingly important to understand the roles they play in supporting school improvement.

This book takes a close look at coaching within one small public high school in New York City, Park East High School. While we focus on the work of one coach, our goal is not to present her work as a model, but rather to develop an understanding of coaching as a professional practice, addressing questions such as these: What strategies does a coach engage to initiate her work with the school community? What are the habits and practices of coaching that effectively support individual teachers and administrators, as well as positive school change? How does the practice of coaching develop over time within a school? How does a coach become a part of the school community and still retain an outsider perspective useful to the community's development?

While the individual person in the coach's role is integral to that picture, our subject is coaching, not the coach. Effective coaching emerges through the interaction and relationships between and among the coach and the teachers and administrators with whom she works. While the coach often initiates these interactions and relationships, we argue that effective coaching depends on the emergence of reciprocity between coach and individual teachers. The goal is to foster relationships among the staff members themselves that are positive, collaborative, and focused on problems of teaching and learning—in other words, a professional learning community (Grossman, Wineburg, & Woolworth, 2001; Stevens & Kahne, 2006).

This last point is critical to the development of coaching as a role and resource for school change. No one person on their own can ever make school change occur, whether a skilled coach, talented principal, or teacher of the year. It requires a team effort. The coach's job is to support these people in developing skills, knowledge, and habits of collaboration that will allow the team to develop and sustain itself even after the coach is gone—whether by choice or at the end of project or funding cycle.

Because of our focus on the reciprocity of coaching relationships, we have chosen to look at coaching from multiple perspectives: from that of external researcher (David), that of three teachers who work with the coach (Alexis, Jennie, Joe), and that of the coach herself (Suzy). Through our sharing of perspectives from different roles—and our dialogue across roles—we construct a picture of coaching, grounded in the real life of the school, that is analytical, practical, committed, and reflective.

HOW IS SCHOOL COACHING DEFINED?

Coaching has become an increasingly common strategy for school improvement, employed both by school districts and intermediary organizations that support school change. As coaching becomes more widespread in American schools, it also becomes more varied in the forms it takes. Neufeld and Roper (2003) helpfully distinguish *content* coaching from *change* coaching.

Content coaches work primarily with teachers on improvement related to particular instructional or curricular practices. For instance, in one coaching model, coaching modalities include instructional modeling, joint planning, co-teaching, formal observation and feedback, informal one-on-one coaching, and mentoring (Poglinco et al., 2003). These are consistent with strategies of other coaching models, such as content-focused mathematics coaching described in West and Staub (2003) or literacy coaching in Rodgers and Rodgers (2007).

Change coaches focus their work at the school organizational level, working with principals, other administrators, and teachers to support the implementation of a school change model or set of principles, like those of the Bay Area Coalition of Equitable Schools or the Institute for Student Achievement, which are discussed in this book. A change coach might, for example, work with the administrators to develop a school schedule that allows for common planning time for faculty or help develop a strategy for sustained professional development around identified schoolwide goals.

While it is not uncommon to find both content and change coaches working in the same school—sometimes even in coordination with each other—in practice, coaches must often blend aspects of both roles to be effective: without attention to organizational structures and building culture, instructional change on the classroom level is unlikely; without knowing well individual teachers' classroom practices, schoolwide change in instructional practice is impossible.

THE ISA PRINCIPLES AND ISA COACHES

The Institute for Student Achievement (ISA) is a nonprofit educational intermediary organization based in Lake Success, New York, with a 15-plus year history of providing academic and social support to underserved and underperforming high school students. ISA partners with school districts to start up small high schools and convert large ones into small learning communities (SLC) organized around a set of seven research-based principles that support all students to graduate from high school and succeed in college (see www.studentachievement.org).[*]

Central to the ISA model is a dedicated team of teachers and counselor who work together to plan curriculum, develop structures and interventions to support students' academic and social development, and engage in ongoing professional development and continuous organizational improvement. ISA's instructional principle specifies a college preparatory instructional program, in particular, inquiry-based instruction and literacy and numeracy across the curriculum. (See Appendix for description of the ISA Model and ISA Principles.)

Implementing this set of principles is challenging for schools, especially those transforming an existing culture and organization from one that reflects prevailing norms for public high schools: teachers working largely in isolation from one another, little coordination between teachers and counselors to support students falling through the cracks, and so on. To meet these challenges, ISA provides a number of support mechanisms, including intensive summer and winter institutes, network meetings of school leaders and counselors, and ongoing formative data collection and reporting, including performance assessments and student surveys (Ancess & Gandolfo, 2006).

In the ISA approach, described by ISA CEO Gerry House in an interview, the role of the coach is to work with the principal and team of teachers to help the school implement the ISA Principles. Since the ISA Principles include implementation of a college preparatory instructional program for all students as well as continuous organizational improvement (see Appendix), the coach's role includes aspects of content coaching, such as planning with individual teachers, observing classes and offering feedback, and providing staff development sessions on inquiry or literacy strategies.

Coaching in ISA partner schools also encompasses aspects of change coaching, as the coach works with the principal and others in the school to implement the ISA principle of continuous organizational improvement, such as creating a schedule that allows teams of teachers to meet regularly or figuring out how to use data from the ISA performance assessments to inform teachers' instruction.

Even as they work directly with teachers and principals, Gerry House states, ISA coaches "help the school build its own capacity, the capacity of the principal and the team." Coaching, then, is an ambitious charge,

---

[*]The National Center for Restructuring Education, Schools, and Teaching (NCREST), Teachers College, Columbia University, for which David is a senior research associate, has been ISA's strategic and research partner since the inception of its model for small schools. In this role, NCREST has documented the implementation of the ISA principles in its partner schools, including Park East High School.

especially since ISA coaches work with schools just one day a week during the school year.

COACHING AS A PROFESSIONAL PRACTICE

Coaching is an extraordinarily complex professional practice—one that interacts continuously with other professional roles—teachers, administrators, other coaches, and staff developers—on two levels: teachers' individual instructional practice and schoolwide organization and culture. The school coach manages a number of tensions:

- Being an insider while maintaining the critical, informed perspective of outsider.
- Working with many people while being able to give close attention to individuals.
- Working simultaneously on the individual and organizational levels.
- Modeling action (being a "doer") while supporting others in acting.
- Maintaining a long-term perspective while working productively in the short term.

To work productively within this matrix of tensions is the essence of coaching as a professional practice, which like other professional practices calls for the development and exercise of "knowledge-in-practice" (Schon, 1987). Of course, coaches need to know about curriculum and instruction and managing a classroom. They also need to know about how schools operate. And, critically, coaches need to know what it means to be part of a professional learning community in order to help grow one within the school in which they work.

The coach's role in the school is unique in a number of ways, none more striking than that he or she is physically there just one or two days a week—in Suzy's case, the one day a week typical for ISA coaches was expanded to two in her second year at the principal's request (see Chapter 2). When she is there, she is intensely involved in the hurly-burly of school life—and stays connected when she is not, through e-mail and phone calls. However, unlike the teachers and administrators she works with, most of her time is spent outside the school.

There are any number of trade-offs for the school and coach that derive from this unusual inside-outside role. The time outside the school allows the coach to connect with external resources, such as other ISA coaches, ISA and NCREST staff members, district personnel, community organizations and institutions, and so on. Distance can also allow for reflection on the school's progress and needs that would be impossible within the moment-to-moment urgency that characterizes so much of the work within the building.

Being a part-time insider has its costs as well. For example, Suzy often works closely with the faculty-led professional development committee in planning a schoolwide professional development sessions, but because of the schedule for coaching days and professional development days, will not then not be present for the meeting itself. Even this seeming disadvantage can be leveraged in the development of teachers on the committee who facilitate the sessions as teacher leaders, or what Suzy terms "schoolwide people."

In her coaching, Suzy works with nearly everyone in the school, from the principal and AP (assistant principal) to the teachers and counselors to the students (she co-leads an advisory group). This might include working in areas that are not typical for school coaches. In one of the brief images that opened this chapter, the coach is seen working with the school's new physical education teacher. While most of her coaching with teachers focuses on the core academic disciplines, Suzy recognized an opportunity to transform the large phys ed class, which was created as a kind of catchall to allow for smaller-sized academic classes, into another site for instruction.

This emphasis on bringing out instructional possibilities throughout the school was one of Suzy's priorities from the very beginning of her coaching at Park East—breaking away from the reality in the school in those days, and in many schools, of "dead" periods and zones throughout the school where little or no teaching and learning is going on. As Suzy says, "A good school is one where good teaching is going on everywhere, all day."

The coach works on multiple levels at once, in particular on those we have termed *individual* and *organizational*. In the chapters that follow, we will describe how the coach works with individual teachers to help them develop their instructional practices. We will also discuss how she works with the school's administration to help to plan for how the school's resources can be best used to respond to needs and support the school's goals.

While it may seem relatively simple to describe the former as individual-level work and the latter as organizational, the distinction is trickier in practice. In fact, the coach is nearly always working on both levels at once, though one may be foregrounded in the specific coaching activity. For example, helping Jennie, a new teacher, develop a unit plan on economics may also contribute to the development of a potential "schoolwide person" to emerge. Conversely, in working with the administration on budgeting for materials or how to plan a staff retreat, the coach is considering how the organizational decisions will affect the individual teachers (and students) in classrooms—in Suzy's words, "making the school safe for teaching."

The role often forces the coach to choose between being a doer or facilitator of others. In a school with so many immediate needs, how does someone with Suzy's skills and experience make the decision when to support, remind, and cajole others to take on the task—or follow through with one they committed to earlier—and when to just do it herself, for example, put together the proposal for a pending grant proposal? As Suzy's experience suggests, there are few if any fixed rules for making such decisions.

Coaching, in many models, is meant to be a temporary support—in the ISA model this has meant coaches working with schools until there is a graduating class from the inception of the intervention. For this reason, the coach is aware of how her work functions in the moment—helping a teacher prepare for the first reading assignment of this semester or working with the Student Life Committee on planning a school ice skating trip is also part of preparing the school to work effectively without her. In Suzy's coaching, the emphasis on developing schoolwide people is a critical aspect of developing capacity within the school to support teaching and learning, as is the emphasis on structures that can channel that support, such as the teacher-led professional development committee and regular full-faculty professional development meetings.

Coaching, like all professional practices, involves the exercise of professional judgment, which itself comes from acting and reflecting—on successes as well as setbacks and missteps. In this book, we argue for the critical importance of reflection to the development of effective coaching—self-reflection, certainly, but also of reaching out to others *within and outside* the school community to engage their perspectives on the role he or she is playing and how he or she can play it more effectively (see Chapter 8).

WHAT ARE THE HABITS OF COACHING?

Coaching knowledge becomes visible through a wide range of what we term *coaching habits*, identifiable ways of interacting with practitioners that create the context for specific actions taken by the teachers and administrators that will contribute to school change and professional learning. These habits—what Dewey (1916) would call active "intellectual dispositions"—are meant to disrupt the deeply engrained social and organizational norms prevalent in schools—from the daily schedule to the way desks are arranged within a classroom to the topics of discussion in the faculty room—a "grammar" (Tyack & Cuban, 1997) that is often counterproductive to effective teaching and learning (Sizer, 1984).

Throughout this book we identify many recurring habits within the different contexts of the coach's work. Some of those that we might call "meta-habits," or those that pervade all of her work as a coach, are:

- Working through relationships.
- Working on multiple levels at once.
- Working deliberately and planfully.
- Working collaboratively.
- Working in the open.

We describe the meta-habits below. In Figure 1.1 we provide a chart that summarizes the many "micro-habits" of coaching and identifies the chapters in which each is treated in detail. While we organize these micro-habits according to the meta-habits, leaving aside "working on multiple levels," in practice most do double or triple duty.

Working Through Relationships

Developing a school culture that emphasizes collaboration depends on developing strong relationships among practitioners, and relationships take time to develop. Many of the stories we recount in this book testify to the coach's belief in forging strong personal relationships with practitioners and being patient and continuing to chip away in working with teachers and administrators. In Chapter 2, we will see how one key relationship helped Suzy to "crack open" a school resistant to collaboration and change. And several teacher accounts in Chapter 4 demonstrate how an initial resistance to being coached became a productive relationship, ultimately leading to fundamental changes in the teachers' instructional practices.

Working on Multiple Levels at Once

While some of the coach's practices focus on the work of individual teachers or focus on the organization of the school, coaching constantly finds and creates ways for these levels to interact. While coaching an individual teacher one-on-one, Suzy is looking for ways in which the teacher and her work can contribute to building a stronger professional community. For example, the co-planning of a unit Suzy and Jennie undertake, described in Chapter 4, connects to a presentation during a schoolwide

Figure 1.1. Habits of Coaching with Chapter References

Working Through Relationships
- Identifying potential teacher leaders—Chapters 2, 7
- Sharing enthusiasm—Chapters 2, 3, 4, 5, 6
- Checking in—Chapters 2, 3, 6, 7
- Being flexible—Chapters 3, 7
- Persisting—Chapters 4, 8
- Building incrementally—Chapter 4

Working Collaboratively
- Modeling the norms for collaboration—Chapters 2, 7
- Offering and inviting feedback—Chapters 3, 6, 7, 8
- Modeling facilitation—Chapters 6, 7

Working Deliberately and Planfully
- Looking for entry points—Chapters 2, 3
- Looking for levers for change—Chapters 2, 3
- Using tools—Chapters 2, 6, 7
- Resourcing—Chapters 2, 3, 4
- Nailing down the details—Chapters 3, 6, 7
- Writing it down—Chapters 3, 7
- Balancing priorities—Chapters 3, 7, 8
- Pushing for student products—Chapters 4, 5
- Framing questions—Chapters 4, 5, 6, 7
- Outlining the course/project—Chapters 4, 5
- Problem-solving—Chapters 4, 6, 7
- Setting achievable targets—Chapters 5, 7
- Recycling—Chapters 3, 5
- Clarifying goals—Chapters 6, 7

Working in the Open
- Pushing for structures that support collaboration—Chapters 2, 7
- Communicating regularly and openly—Chapters 2, 3, 4, 7
- Making connections, sharing strengths—Chapters 2, 3, 4, 5, 6
- Expanding inclusion—Chapter 2
- Reflecting systematically—Chapters 3, 7, 8
- Debriefing—Chapters 5, 6

professional development session. Conversely, the coach's work with the ninth-grade team on reorganizing the afterschool program led to opportunities for teachers to develop their individual instructional practice (see Chapter 2).

Working Deliberately and Planfully

As the image we begin with of Suzy running into Joe in the hallway suggests, Suzy's coaching, while opportunistic, reveals an emphasis on plans, lists, and being "concrete." While this emphasis does not discount the value of being spontaneous, it does demonstrate a habit that is both essential to Suzy in how she thinks about and organizes her coaching and one she continually seeks to develop in others, especially those who are taking or may take on schoolwide leadership roles. For Suzy, everything is planned, and the act of planning is itself a hallmark of professional community. Developing such a habit is particularly challenging in schools like the Park East High School she first encountered, where the dominant mode of dealing with problems was reactive rather than planful.

Working Collaboratively

As Joe points out in Chapter 4, Suzy constantly looks for opportunities to bring people together to share ideas and resources, offer feedback, and solve problems. She facilitates the collaboration of others, for example, in how she paired up Ed Poli and Brianne Tafuro in one of the opening vignettes; works collaboratively with others, for example, as a member of a committee; and models collaboration in how she facilitates and participates. In Chapter 3, we examine how these habits become visible in how Suzy structures her coaching and the practices that recur. And in Chapter 6, we describe how collaboration in supporting school leaders often means taking a back seat rather than driving the boat.

Working in the Open

Schools are often places in which professionals who should be collaborating instead work in isolation and even at odds from one another. Decisions are made with little input from teachers. Teachers are wary to allow colleagues or administrators into their classrooms. There is a pervasive distrust of other's intentions or motivations. Such conditions were certainly evident at Park East when Suzy began coaching there, as we describe in Chapter 2. In order to be able to work with the many people she must to be effective, coaching must be visibly and emphatically open in how it operates. Suzy's emphasis on making decisions openly and inclusively, getting input from and posting minutes of meetings to the entire professional community, and reflecting on every meeting and professional development session all serve the double purpose of making her own work possible and helping to change the culture of the school to one in which collaboration prevails.

WHY FOCUS ON ONE COACH AND ONE SCHOOL?

Coaching is not only complex but intensely context-bound. Our goal in this book is not to identify a set of strategies that are easily transferable to any such school, although we hope readers will discover useful strategies here. Instead we try to provide a close-up of coaching within an actual school, with its unique conditions, needs, and cast of characters, to describe how the coach and the schoolpeople with whom he or she works understand the practice of coaching.

We focused on Park East High School and Suzy Ort's coaching for a number of reasons. Coaching at Park East is neither strictly content-oriented or change-oriented, but rather coaching on multiple levels, both the individual and the organizational. As we stated above, these two levels cannot be isolated in practice, since they continually interact and influence each other. Park East provided us a site to examine how these aspects of coaching can be integrated.

Park East also provided us a site for looking at how coaching develops over time. Suzy was the first ISA coach at Park East and continued to coach there for 5 years, working with two principals and many teachers. After her fifth year of coaching, she became a part-time assistant principal of the school. Chapter 2 provides an overview of how coaching looks in different stages of the school's development; later chapters, especially Chapters 5, 6, and 7, provide images of how coaching looks within a school that is becoming a true professional community.

Changing the culture of an existing school, large or small, is a daunting challenge (Fullan, 1993). By focusing on the coaching within a single school engaged within such a cultural transformation, we hoped to provide useful lessons for schools that face similar challenges and the coaches and organizations that work with these schools.

To be able to affect the culture of the schools in which they work, coaches need to enter into that culture and that community. As we describe in Chapter 2, Suzy initiated her coaching through one-on-one work with individual teachers open to getting help with their classroom instruction. This is just one of many "entry points" ISA guides its coaches to identify and engage over time to encourage change. Entry points may appear suddenly, as in the vignette above, in which Ed sits next to Suzy at a meeting and she encourages him to work with Brianne on her poster projects, but are also created within the context of collaborative planning with teachers around their instruction (see Chapter 4) or with school leaders around organizational issues (see Chapters 6 and 7).

WHO ARE THE AUDIENCES FOR THE BOOK?

As a study of one school, our book is not intended to provide a definitive picture of coaching. Our hope is that the habits we identify and contextualize will be of interest and use to coaches, school leaders, and organizations that support coaching, as well as to contribute to more research on school coaching. And while we describe coaching for whole-school change, the habits and practices we identify will be relevant and useful to content coaching as well.

Coaching works when it brings people in multiple roles within and outside the school into collaboration. For this reason, we believe a book about school coaching will be of interest and, we hope, of use to a range of audiences. For all readers, we hope that the book will contribute to a deeper, more nuanced understanding of how coaching functions as a professional practice within the life of a school. However, readers in different roles *vis-à-vis* coaching may find somewhat different purposes—and may use the book somewhat differently:

For *teachers*, the book may serve as a kind of user's guide to coaching, providing ideas and images that expand their thinking about how to work with the coach and get the most out of coaching for your own professional development.

For *school administrators*, the book may help you broaden your knowledge of how coaches work on different levels. It may be especially helpful in figuring out how to work with coaches to develop the habits and structures that contribute to a collaborative school culture, one focused on continually improving teaching and learning.

For *organizations* that employ and support coaches, the book may clarify the habits and practices coaches bring and develop so that you can more effectively support your coaches in developing these habits and applying them to advance your goals for school change. The stories and vignettes in Chapters 4 and 6 may serve as material for text-based discussions on how coaching can support teachers' instructional planning and the development of a professional learning community within the school.

For *researchers*, the book represents a particular methodological approach to studying coaching: a single case study constructed from multiple perspectives and multiple roles. From the data, we have developed a set of coaching habits that could be applied as an analytical frame within or across other school coaching settings. Given the complexity of coaching, our understanding of coaching will only benefit from a wide range of complementary methods and analyses.

Finally, for *coaches* themselves, our book may provide some new strategies and ways to approach coaching problems; however, it may be most useful in providing images of how coaching develops over time—and a reminder to not give up when the going gets tough!

HOW IS THE BOOK ORGANIZED?

As we stated above, the book is not intended as a comprehensive account of how Park East developed or a catalog of all of the coaching actions that have taken place there in the 5 years we have been involved with the school. Instead, we focus on specific moments from the life of the school during that period to illuminate the nature of coaching practice.

However, we felt that it is important to begin by providing context for the coaching moments and our analysis of them. For this reason, in Chapter 2 we describe how Suzy initiated her coaching relationship with the school and how her coaching has changed its focus over her 5 years in the role.

In Chapter 3, we provide two lenses for examining coaching: first, by illustrating how Suzy organizes her coaching time over a typical week; second, through describing the key coaching practices that fill that time. The chapter includes artifacts from Suzy's work that bring to life both what was planned and what actually happened.

In Chapter 4, we zoom in on a critical component of coaching, planning instructional units with teachers. We share several planning stories, and consider the role planning plays in the development over time of teachers' practices.

While planning is the central practice of coaching, it relates strongly to a number of other practices that we consider in Chapter 5. These include observing teachers' classroom instruction, providing external resources, and regularly checking in with the teachers and administrators with whom the coach works about where they are, what they need, and how they feel—an emotional side of coaching that is often overlooked.

Chapter 6 shifts us from the individual instructional to the organizational level, illustrating how coaching seeks to develop habits and practices of a professional learning community. Again, we include a number of stories to provide images of what a developing professional community does and looks like.

Chapter 7 focuses on how coaching works with and supports the development of school leadership, both established leaders—the principal and assistant principal—and emerging teacher leaders.

Finally, in Chapter 8, we step back and reflect on some of the challenges and possibilities of school coaching, offering, we hope, lessons for coaches, school leaders, and teachers who have the opportunity to collaborate in a coaching relationship.

HOW WAS THE BOOK MADE?

This book grew out of a pilot study on coaching at Park East conducted by David. In the study, he shadowed Suzy on two typical coaching days, observing her interactions with teachers, administrators, groups (such as in Professional Development and Student Life committee meetings), students, school secretaries, and so on. From these data, he identified a number of "generative moments" and conducted interviews with teachers and administrators involved and with the coach.

The data from just a few days was so rich that David and Suzy decided to collaborate on a resource on coaching that would reach a broader audience. Because the teachers' perspectives from the interviews had been so important in understanding the dimensions of coaching, they invited three teachers who had been involved in the pilot study to be co-authors and share their perspectives on coaching.

The book project grew through continued observations and interviews discussions between David and Suzy; and discussions during writers' retreats among all of us. From all of these discussions and data, David developed the analytical frame for the book, based on identification of key coaching habits, and the narrative frame for each chapter.

All of the collaborators have read and discussed the entire contents of the book, offering input and feedback. The picture of coaching in a small school that emerges, as fostering the habits of collaboration, is the product of our own collaborative experience.

In many places, these collaborators speak directly to the reader. For example, in Chapter 2, Suzy describes how she structures her work and the major coaching practices she uses regularly; in Chapter 4, Alexis, Jennie, and Joe describe their experiences in planning instruction with the coach; in Chapter 6, Alexis describes her collaboration with Suzy on a schoolwide committee; and in Chapter 8, each contributor reflects on lasting lessons about the coaching relationship.

CHAPTER 2

The Development of Coaching over Time

This chapter tells the story of how coaching at Park East High School got started and how the coaching and the school have changed over time. The chapter provides organizational context that will be of particular interest for school leaders as they consider critical questions about initiating coaching within their schools. It should also be of interest to coaches themselves, if for no other reason than to reassure them that the difficult, often lonely work of a coach can contribute to real change and even noticeable results—in teachers' instruction as well as the climate and organization of the school. Other readers may choose to skip this chapter, at least for now, and jump to Chapter 3, which begins a detailed examination of coaching habits and practices.

We begin the story with brief portraits of the school and the coach as they were at the beginning of the coaching relationship. From there we describe three stages of coaching: (1) initiating coaching; (2) building structures and developing habits; and (3) deepening quality and responsiveness. While these stages build upon one another, they are also fluid and overlapping. For example, in Stage 1, which corresponds to the first year of Suzy's work with the school, Suzy worked individually with a number of teachers on planning instruction; 3 years later, in Stage 3, she is still planning instruction with teachers; however, now she focuses on new teachers while facilitating support from disciplinary specialists for more experienced teachers with whom she previously had worked more closely.

We describe Stage 3 as the last stage of coaching, roughly encompassing Suzy's fourth and fifth year working with the school. However, this does not mean that there is no need for a Stage 4. While many school change coaching models are temporary, focused on the implementation of a particular instructional or organizational model, we argue in Chapter 8 that *coaching*, if not an individual coach, should play an ongoing role within the organization and cultural life of a school.

At the conclusion of each section, we identify some of the coaching habits that are critical to coaching effectiveness in this stage. Many of these habits will reappear in different contexts throughout the book.

THE SCHOOL

Park East is a small high school in East Harlem. Just blocks away from Central Park East Secondary School, which under Deborah Meier's leadership had achieved status as a national model of secondary school reform, Park East had accumulated a history of low academic achievement. In October 2002, when Suzy Ort was matched with Park East High School for her coaching assignment, the school had 342 students and 24 teachers. Ninety-six percent of the student population was African American or Hispanic, and 77% of all students were eligible for free or reduced lunch—in reality, the poverty rate was likely even higher. The school's graduation rate that year was a dismal 31%, 27 percentage points lower than the city average.

Park East was a transfer school within the New York City's Alternative High School Superintendency. The purpose of transfer schools was and is to enroll students who fail elsewhere. Nick Mazzarella, who had been appointed principal just months before Suzy's assignment, supported the school's transformation, consistent with changes within the DOE (Department of Education), to a regular high school admitting students directly out of junior high school—a goal that was largely realized in his three years as principal.

Mazzarella's first concern was creating a safer, more orderly school climate for teachers and students. He focused on making sure that students were in classrooms instead of roaming the halls. What happened within classrooms was less clear, as he encountered a faculty suspicious of administrators and used to working in virtual isolation. As Joe recalls, teachers regularly locked their doors while class was in session—not to keep students in but to keep administrators, along with late-coming students, out.

Instruction at the school was largely teacher directed and driven by textbooks. In general, teaching was characterized by "one-shot-deal" lessons with little emphasis on extended writing or reading, processes for developing and revising work, or multistep projects.

The one common goal of all teachers was to get as many students as possible to pass the Regents examinations required for graduation. Joe recounts how the focus on test preparation, along with the high student absenteeism, shaped his practice:

> In my first two years of teaching, I would often recycle lessons from Monday to Tuesday—there would be so many new faces in the class on Tuesday who had missed Monday's lesson and many of the students

who were there on Monday needed me to reteach the topic anyway. In terms of the Regents, the big push was to get the students to complete the test, as many would leave large portions of the test blank.

Nor was there much support for new teachers in developing instructional practice. Alexis describes her first-year teaching assignment, which included four sections of living environment and one of earth science:

> I was the only first-year teacher in the department and I was told by a senior member of the department that he would not teach earth science because he had no experience with the content. Well, the only experience I had with earth science was the general science class I took my freshman year of high school. At least he had experience with teaching that I didn't. So I sucked it up, got the earth science review book, and taught right out of that. And from what I could tell I was not the only one using review books as textbooks.

NEW PARTNERSHIPS

When Nick Mazzarella arrived at the school, Park East was already working with the Institute for Student Achievement (ISA) through its STAR (Success Through Academic Readiness) program, which supported a small group of students with extra support, including tutoring and counseling. The program was largely successful with the small group of students targeted, but was not intended to have an impact on the school as a whole—any collaboration with Park East teachers was informal. As ISA phased out the STAR program in all schools, it offered Park East the opportunity to join several other STAR schools in participating in its new model, which envisioned whole-school change consistent with its research-based principles, including a college preparatory curriculum for all students, rich in opportunities for inquiry-based instruction and literacy and numeracy across the curriculum; extended-day and -year learning opportunities; and "distributed counseling," in which teachers and counselors work as a team to support students' academic success, social-emotional development, and college readiness. (See the Appendix for the complete ISA principles.)

Mazzarella saw the partnership with ISA as a resource in his goal of transforming Park East into a "regular" high school. He committed the school, beginning with the ninth grade, to transform grade by grade over 4 years to a college preparatory high school. He was introduced to Suzy in May 2002, just before the upcoming ISA Summer Institute, and decided that she would be a good match as the school's ISA coach.

Events before and during Suzy's first year of coaching suggested that this would not be an easy enterprise. For example, just one teacher from the newly formed ninth-grade team of six—a new math teacher hired from the ISA program staff—attended the ISA summer institute before the first year of the new program. Perhaps more troubling, Beth (a pseudonym), the veteran teacher Nick assigned to serve as coordinator for the ninth-grade Transition Academy, resisted the idea of regular collaborative team meetings, a cornerstone of the ISA model. Teachers assigned to the new ninth-grade academy viewed the ISA program with skepticism, often locking their doors to signal their attitude toward it—and, by extension, to the new coach. To make matters worse, the five staff members affiliated with the terminating ISA program experienced disappointment and even anger at losing their program, which led to a degree of antagonism to the new whole-school approach. Subsequently, several of the ISA program staff transitioned to become Park East staff members, including a guidance counselor, Shernell Thomas, and a college advisor, Marica Edmonds.

THE COACH

To these challenges, Suzy Ort brought a varied background to her coaching. Before becoming a school coach with the ISA, she had taught social studies at University Heights High School, a small alternative high school in the Bronx. As part of her teaching, she had also facilitated a "family group," an hourlong daily class addressing socioemotional issues and supporting academic growth for the school's highly disaffected students. For 2 years (and several summers) she served as a teacher at a language school in Prague, from where her parents had immigrated to the United States 30 years earlier.

Suzy was motivated to take on the role of school coach for a number of reasons. She had recently completed her doctorate at Teachers College, Columbia University, where she had been a research assistant at the National Center for Restructuring Education, Schools, and Teaching (NCREST) on several studies and educational research projects, including ones documenting the development of small high schools. When ISA engaged NCREST as its research partner to collaborate on coaching and other aspects of the new model, co-director Jackie Ancess recommended to ISA that Suzy be one of the first ISA school coaches, each of whom would work with their school one day a week.

Gerry House, the CEO of ISA, has stated that ISA sought coaches with strong instructional backgrounds. She added, "The ISA principles are not implemented in a linear fashion. It's the simultaneous implementation of all the principles that produces the outcomes. I believe that if schools begin with the implementation of the college preparatory instructional program the necessity for the other principles will emerge."

Suzy recalls her interest in the new position and, for her, new challenge:

> Coaching appealed to me because I could use some of the research and analytic skills I had developed in graduate school as I worked with the principal to improve the school. . . . I was eager to test out some of the ideas I had been researching and writing about back in the school setting. . . . It also appealed to my knowledge of and deep interest in curriculum developed during my time as a teacher in high school and in graduate school.

Suzy had another, more practical motivation to take on the one-day-a-week coaching job; as the mother of two small children, coaching suited her desire to work part-time.

STAGE 1—INITIATING COACHING

Suzy initiated her new role of coach by "going into a school and working with people to engage them in talking about their practice to help improve the instructional practice of the school." As stated above, ISA expects coaches to begin with the implementation of the college preparatory instructional program.

The Lay of the Land

The summer before she was to begin as its coach, Suzy was introduced by Jackie Ancess and Gerry House to Nick Mazzarella, who had recently been appointed principal of Park East. In beginning her work with the school, Suzy saw her first task as trying to "understand the lay of the land . . . just figuring out how the school operated politically, who had power, who didn't, what was important, how did it run? In a place like Park East, it was very problematic as those things are not apparent."

Nick had developed a strong relationship with Beth, the ninth-grade Transition Academy coordinator and the school's programmer (who created the teachers' and students' class schedules). This meant that if Suzy was to reach the ninth-grade teachers, she would have to work with Beth. The obvious way to achieve this would be through regular team meetings that focused on the ISA principles, especially the ISA principle of college preparatory instruction. However, as Suzy recounts, Nick, Beth, and

Van (a pseudonym), the assistant principal, "actively didn't want to have meetings. It was dangerous because the value of collaboration and the value of teachers being at the table and having discussion and coming to a decision and sticking to it were antithetical to the way things had been done at Park East. Everything was done behind closed doors."

This was not surprising, Suzy recognized, since Nick was himself just beginning to develop relationships with teachers in a school that had a history of teacher–administration tension and distrust. Beth's role was also a factor in the tense professional climate. Joe, while not on the ninth-grade team at the time, observed the degree of "intimidation and fear" that she inspired in teachers. Suzy described the professional climate of the school at the time as "toxic."

Denied access to teachers through establishing team meetings, Suzy sought other ways to develop relationships with members of the ninth-grade team, while not losing sight of the goal to work with the team as a whole. "The main thing was to keep my eyes open and watching, while developing relationships with people, figuring out who I could trust, who would be willing to work with me, who would be a key 'informant' in sort of anthropological terms. I felt that I really needed to have some allies. First I had to have people I could talk to."

Giving Tips and Making Allies

In the first several months, Suzy focused on developing relationships, in an intentionally low-key manner, with those teachers she felt would be open to working on instructional changes they could make in their own classroom, often sharing tips from her own teaching, such as the use of various competitive review games and the idea of organizing a class into stations students cycle through to participate in different tasks and activities.

While she was well received by individual teachers and felt she was offering useful advice, Suzy was also developing allies in reaching the whole school culture and organization. With this goal in mind, she focused her attention on two stronger teachers who were well respected by their colleagues, John Giambalvo, a social studies teacher, and Dyanand Sugrim, a science teacher. Suzy saw both as potential teacher leaders. John, especially, turned out to be the key ally she needed; he served both as "informant," helping Suzy understand the power dynamics of the school, and also as an entry point to the rest of the faculty, based on his own relationships and credibility with other teachers.

Consistent with her approach that year, Suzy's relationship with John began with a focus on his classroom. For example, Suzy worked with him to develop "one big idea" for his class overall as well as for each class period, in addition to the more traditional textbook-based instruction, which was tightly focused on questions with single answers. "He was incredibly open to having someone in his classroom." The two worked together on a 6-week project to prepare the ninth-grade students to argue the issue of rent stabilization during a mock City Council hearing at City Hall. Suzy helped John plan the project and develop questions students would research, for example, "How would the end of rent stabilization affect New York's economy?" Planning such projects with teachers would become a core coaching strategy, one we examine in detail in Chapter 4.

Over several months, their conversations—in person and over e-mail—expanded from a focus on John's classroom instruction to considering possibilities for collaboration on the ninth-grade team. These conversations represented Suzy's first steps in moving from focusing on the individual instructional level to addressing teamwide issues related to instruction. She described her early interactions with John this way:

> Our conversations were focused on his classroom practices and then shifted to how to develop a professional learning community among the faculty that would have similar conversations about teaching practices to those we were having: what habits did individuals need to have to do this schoolwide; what schoolwide structures needed to exist—such as regular meetings focusing on instruction; how could we contribute to the trusting relationships that have to exist among faculty members as precursor to deep conversations?

Pushing to Meet

In early November of that first year, Suzy judged that enough trust existed between her and at least some of the ninth-grade team members to press for regular team meetings in order to tackle the ISA principles in a more systematic fashion. Beth held meetings of the ninth-grade Transitions Academy; however, these were largely devoted to discussing individual students identified for additional support. Suzy arranged with Beth to schedule additional *voluntary* team meetings, then asked John to reach out to other staff members and enlist their support, or at least their presence, at meetings. John agreed, and, Suzy recalls, "It worked. He brought everyone to a first meeting of the ninth-grade team."

Suzy and John's insider-outsider alliance was successful in bringing a wary faculty, used to top-down, bureaucratic staff meetings, to the table. Being at the table, though, was still a far cry from the kind of collaborative professional community Suzy envisioned. To her frustration, the first meetings, co-planned by her with Beth, dealt almost exclusively with logistics, for example, putting together supply lists. The first opportunity to engage in a discussion of instructional goals related to the ISA principles came at the fourth team meeting, when the school counselor recommended the team read and discuss an article from her graduate course about strategies for fostering student metacognition. While the discussion, in Suzy's opinion, was hardly "terrific" in terms of depth or practical applications to the classroom, several teachers e-mailed Suzy to say they had enjoyed the discussion of the article.

The positive response suggested an entry point for more collaboration and discussion of instructional issues. John suggested capitalizing on this minor flurry of e-mails by expanding their e-mail correspondence into a voluntary whole-staff listserv. He set up the listserv, and its use grew steadily, fed by regular contributions from Suzy (including detailed minutes she kept of team meetings). At one point during the first year, Suzy noted, everyone on the team (with one exception, Beth, the team leader, who did not use e-mail) took part in an e-mail discussion at least once. While Nick did not post to the listserv, he read the e-mails and commended the coach on what was happening—the first positive feedback she received from the principal.

Team meetings became more regular, though still treated as an add-on to the teachers' regular work: the meetings were held during teachers' lunchtime since there were no dedicated times for team meetings in the schedule. Suzy describes the meetings at this point as loosely planned; she did most of the facilitation—at times, Beth would "pipe in." There was little attention yet to developing agendas that reflected teachers' concerns or goals related to the ISA principles, and Suzy was still keeping and sending out the minutes, but the norm of meeting to talk about instructional issues had been initiated.

In Through Afterschool

Another opportunity to address instruction came during a team meeting with the discussion of afterschool tutoring, which had been initiated as a way to use the discretionary funds provided by ISA to implement its principles, specifically the principle of extended day learning opportunities. ISA's budgeting process required expenditures to be explicitly linked to the ISA principles and the specific learning goals the school had established in relation to the principles. Since no such goals existed yet at Park East, Suzy saw the budgeting process as a possible lever to encourage the team to establish some instructional goals and ways to meet them, beginning with the afterschool program.

While teachers began to offer afterschool tutoring and were compensated from the ISA funds, students were not showing up in significant numbers. Again, John played a critical role in making this a whole-team issue and an early opportunity for collaboration around teaching and learning issues. His frustration with the small student turnout for his own afterschool tutoring led him to suggest to Suzy putting the issue of student participation on the agenda for a team meeting and to consider other ways the afterschool program might be reorganized.

"This was an opening for us," Suzy recalls. "We decided [as a team] that people would teach what they wanted in the extended day program to a limited number of kids. We discussed activities for an afterschool program. There were about ten people there; everyone came up with one. One person decided to do a choir; other suggestions were a *Jeopardy*-like game, a science club, and Latin dance." She recalled the discussions about the afterschool program as one of the key opportunities to crack open the school to change: "This is the first time we had a concept—that afterschool is to be different [from regular classes] and highly engaging for the kids to get them to stay for an extra hour."

One of the afterschool sessions was planned, at Suzy's suggestion, by Dyanand Sugrim as a way to give students real laboratory experience they were not getting in their science classes due to lack of materials and equipment and a focus on textbook-driven, Regents-exam-prep instruction. In the Dissection Club, Dyanand worked with a group of about 15 students, and often with Suzy as well, to perform dissections of increasingly complex organisms, culminating in a fetal pig, each time filling out a laboratory write-up sheet on what they learned.

With each new organism, students' enthusiasm built. Students attended regularly and took their work seriously. When Suzy saw what was happening, she encouraged other teachers and administrators in the school to drop by the club meetings as a way of sharing images of successful practice and building momentum within the faculty for instructional change. Teachers saw their own students working in ways that some had not thought possible.

"Dissection worked—we had a success," Suzy recounts. "We started to pay attention to what was working, what wasn't, and why. . . . Afterschool was the thing that really kicked us off." The afterschool program provided an early and visible example of how careful planning of instructional units and projects can lead to improved student results, both in their work and their behavior. This emphasis on planning projects would become a hallmark of Suzy's instructional coaching, as we describe in Chapter 4.

Dissection Club also provided the whole team with a tangible success that came out of a collaborative process. For Suzy, this represented an important turning point in her work on the organizational level—one she hoped to build on in the second year. Even some of the less successful afterschool ventures pointed to positive developments within the faculty. Suzy comments, "John's *Jeopardy* activity failed but he wanted it to work. I told him to drop it and move on. It took him three weeks but he did it. It was one of the first times that when something was not working, it became acceptable to admit it, scrap it, and move on." In Suzy's mind, this was laying the groundwork for a professional norm of honest assessment of the quality of practice.

Critical Moments, Crucial Support

During this stage, there were many times when Suzy and Nick's relationship became strained. Throughout, ISA and NCREST provided Suzy with the "support and insight" she needed to continue functioning in her role as coach. Gerry House and Jackie Ancess met with Nick on a number of occasions during the first year to clarify the ISA model and lend Suzy their unequivocal support as the school's ISA coach.

Equally important, from Suzy's perspective, were the frequent conversations she had with Jackie Ancess, who would debrief Suzy's coaching experiences with her and provide reassurance about the process. Suzy comments, "Jackie would constantly remind me that conflict was part of the process of developing a trusting relationship with Nick and others at the school. She encouraged me to recognize moments of conflict, share them, get passed them, and move on."

Coaching Habits Examined

At this initial stage of coaching, habits emphasize building relationships, seeking entry points to the professional culture, and modeling norms of collaboration. Some of the specific coaching habits evident here are:

- *Identifying potential teacher leaders*, especially, at this stage, John Giambalvo, and later, Joe, Alexis, and others.
- *Looking for entry points* for discussing instruction, for instance, the early discussion of an article. Identifying and engaging entry points is a principle of ISA's approach to coaching.
- *Looking for levers for change*, for example, the ISA budgeting process leveraged a discussion of how to structure the extended-day program.
- *Pushing for structures that support collaboration*, including regular team meetings as envisioned in the ISA Model and the establishment of a faculty listserv.

- *Communicating regularly and openly,* including getting input on agendas, sharing minutes from meetings.
- *Sharing enthusiasm* over early successes, such as the Dissection Club.

STAGE 2—BUILDING STRUCTURES AND DEVELOPING HABITS

The first year of Suzy's coaching at Park East was winding down with
some hard-won successes, including regular team meetings, the extended-
day afterschool program (especially the success of Dissection Club), and
regular teamwide communication on the listserv. Now it was time to build
on these accomplishments and expand the work to more of the faculty. On
paper, the second year would focus on developing a tenth-grade team as
the next step in the year-by-year progression to full-school implementation of the ISA principles; for a small school like Park East, this would
involve most of the school's faculty. The opportunity for coaching to reach
nearly all the teachers in the school came quickly as the second ISA summer institute approached.

Planting the Carrot Seed: Getting People Talking

The ISA Summer Institute that year took place over 5 days immediately
after the school year ended, and was held at a bucolic conference center
on the North Shore of Long Island. The 5 days were structured to provide
time and support for teachers to work in discipline groups developing
inquiry-based curricular lessons and units (administrators met with their
counterparts during this time). The institute also provided daily blocks of
team time dedicated to school-based planning.

In contrast to the previous year's experience, Park East planned to
send a team of 12 to the institute, which included most of the ninth- and
tenth-grade teachers, Nick, and Van, the assistant principal. Suzy and John
Giambalvo took the initiative to make sure there was a plan for how to use
team time; and an agenda was developed, with some input from teachers,
by Nick, Van, John, and Suzy—Beth had made it clear that she did not
work during the summer. Suzy recalls her goal for developing professional
community at the time: "I just wanted to get groups of people talking
about something—I didn't care what about." The point was to develop a
habit of communicating as a faculty.

The agenda they came up with was intended to support the Park
East team in gaining a better understanding of the ISA principles and
then identifying some concrete ways to implement them—a strategy ISA
recommends and provides tools for. Though eager to get to the institute,

Suzy felt some "trepidation" at the loosely developed agenda and shaky support from the administrators:

> At our last team meeting of that year, neither Beth nor Nick showed up, and I ended the meeting by reading *The Carrot Seed*, a children's book about how a whole family tells the youngest member not to bother to plant the carrot seed, that "it won't come up." Yet the boy persists, watering and caring for the seed daily. Ultimately it grows into a fine, huge carrot and the father, mother, and older brother regret their earlier disbelief. Over pizza, I compared the efforts of our team to the little boy and the carrot seed.

Despite Suzy's concerns, the Park East team time got off to a good start. Teachers were excited to have a chance to relate to one another outside of school walls. During unscheduled times there was racquetball playing and hanging out in the hot tub or at the pub.

Van facilitated most of the sessions, which Suzy interpreted as a hopeful sign as it showed a new level of administrative ownership and involvement with the team's work. While pleased with progress toward the ISA goal of school leaders taking ownership of the team meetings, she felt being sidelined as facilitator a rebuke of sorts to her as the person who had been leading the work of the team all along.

Following the basic agenda the planning group had devised, the team began by examining each ISA principle and then creating a wish list of all that would exist at the school if it were able to realize full implementation. Suzy recalls these as "uplifting and exiting sessions—we joked about 'chills' of excitement and anticipation about the possibilities of change becoming routine."

Working from these lists, the team identified two of the ISA principles that seemed to relate most strongly to their dream plans for the school: ongoing professional development and distributed counseling. To address how these principles could be realized, the team broke up into three "interest groups," each of which would concentrate on an area of school practice:

- The Professional Development group would design and run weekly 50-minute full-faculty professional development meetings.
- The Student Life group would organize schoolwide community-building events such as a student orientation, "Back to School Day," and a Halloween celebration.
- The House group came about because Nick Mazzarella had experience with the "family group" advisory structure from his previous school and wanted something similar at Park East. The group

would oversee the newly created advisory program, which envisioned weekly small-group meetings of teachers with students assigned to their "house."

During the remaining team time, each interest group came up with a concept statement about what their group would be responsible for and what kinds of activities they envisioned for the coming year. Suzy floated among the groups, helping each to formulate plans and establish some organizational norms, such as regular meeting times and having an identified point person. In working with the Student Life working group, she was able to help the committee plan for the first-ever student orientation at Park East; teachers signed up to take responsibility for a particular aspect of its organization and arrive at school prior to opening to make final arrangements. Nick and Van were also available to the groups to respond to questions—most commonly, "What can we buy?"

The institute ended with a ceremony in which each school presented to the others what it had achieved. The Park East staff put together a skit culminating in a human pyramid meant to suggest laying the foundations for change.

Summer Storm

Despite the promise of the first year and the good feeling generated by the summer institute's collaborative work, tension between Suzy and the administrators persisted. Just before departing the institute, Nick and Van pulled Suzy aside to discuss her role in the school next year. Suzy recalls, "It was not a pleasant conversation and a highly confusing one given that the summer institute had been such a hugely positive experience for the whole team. . . . I think it was their way of making sure I did not attribute too much of the positive energy to my efforts or those of ISA so that I continued to remember who was in charge."

For Suzy, the tension reached such a critical level that she felt the need for outside help. She spoke to Jackie Ancess, the NCREST co-director who worked closely with all the ISA coaches, just before leaving for her family's vacation in the Czech Republic, wondering aloud whether she should give up the coaching position at Park East. Jackie counseled Suzy not to make any rash decisions and enjoy her vacation; she could decide when she returned to New York.

Fortunately, a change in district leadership came into play over the summer. Alan Dichter, a former small-school principal, became the Local Instructional Superintendent for Park East. Suzy had a good relationship with Alan, having taught at the school founded by Nancy Mohr, Alan's late wife, and she considered both to be mentors. Alan's support for Suzy bolstered her position with Nick, who sent her an unexpected e-mail to welcome her back to the school, beginning "Guess what? . . . "

Just before school began, Nick asked Suzy to take on an extra day a week at the school, which would be paid for from the school's budget. He told her he needed her help to deepen the work and deal with the demands of the expanded team. Specifically, Nick wanted Suzy to continue her instructional coaching with an expanding number of teachers and work more closely with him and other administrators as the school entered into a new organizational structure being introduced by the DOE, one in which schools were grouped into regions.

If the tension did not all disappear with the midsummer heat, it had at least diminished by the time Suzy was back in the country. Her coaching priority became making the goals and organizational structures planned at the institute a reality.

Back to School

In a fortunate piece of timing, the New York City Department of Education that year instituted 4 days of school-based professional development prior to the start of the school year to address new curriculum mandates. The interest groups, now called *working* groups, met before school opened and discussed how they would use the time to introduce the plans they developed at the institute to the rest of the faculty. While there was a new feeling of teacher ownership, the teachers involved anticipated resistance from colleagues who had not been at the institute.

The working group leaders felt that the faculty might bristle at new demands on teachers and perhaps even perceive an insider group developing among those who took part in the institute—that is, those who were now "in" with the principal and coach. In the event, the plans were received positively by the rest of the faculty but with some wariness. Alexis, who had not been at the institute, felt out of the loop, as though an "in group" was forming.

Joe, not at the institute either, remembers that some teachers, himself included, felt "a need to discuss the plans fully to make them feel like a somewhat democratic choice and not something that was foisted on the many by the few." He recognized, however, that during the first couple of days prior to student arrivals, John and Suzy "did a lot to make the committee structure seem more palatable."

Some of the teachers, especially teachers new to the school, joined the groups; for example, Clancy McKenna, an English teacher, joined

Student Life; Drew Allsopp, another English teacher, joined Professional Development; and Liz Lauben, a science teacher, joined the House working group. Despite her wariness, Alexis joined the Student Life working group: "I made sure to contribute as much as I could to prove my value to the school community."

The next step, in Suzy's mind, involved establishing weekly times for the working groups to meet and plan for the events and practices envisioned in the institute planning. In consultation with Nick and Suzy—and with a good deal of encouragement from them, since there was "not really a rush for the job"—each group had a designated teacher leader, including John for the PD Group, Lisa, a social studies teacher, for Student Life, and Yessenia and Lynnette for the House. Suzy met with each group to develop norms for effective group practice, which included committing to regular meeting times (with reminders sent out regularly to build membership); posting of minutes publicly on the listserv; and regularly requesting feedback from the whole faculty. Suzy viewed these habits as critical to making the groups' work as open, collaborative, and inclusive as possible, to counteract the school's long history of closed-door decisionmaking.

As the school year got under way, Suzy's coaching priorities expanded from working with individual teachers on planning instructional practices to include working with the new working groups; she planned her weekly schedule to participate in as many of the working group meetings as possible (see Chapter 3). The new focus on coaching at the organizational level also affected how Suzy worked with teachers on the individual level: Meeting with the working groups brought her into contact with teachers she had not worked with before, which in some cases led to working with them individually on instruction. She also began to use individual instructional planning time she had with some of the teacher leaders to discuss working group issues. (In Chapter 4, we describe how Suzy's work with Alexis on the Student Life working group provided an entry point into working with her on instruction.)

Online communication continued to be an important means for Suzy to communicate, as well as to develop and deepen relationships, with teachers, especially emerging teacher leaders. For example, the leaders would e-mail Suzy meeting minutes to review before posting them to the listserv. Suzy viewed this as an indication of the leaders' commitment to schoolwide work: "They value the listserv messages they send to their colleagues, and want it to go over well. They see the importance of communicating with the whole faculty. They care about the quality of their work." She also felt a new confidence in the teachers' respect for her opinion, "not only about instructional practices but about schoolwide organizational issues as well." She adds, "They were starting to get what the work was about, what the possibilities of the coaching relationship could be—collaborative, helpful, designed to meet their needs."

The postings invigorated the use of the listserv by the whole faculty, and it continued to develop as an important form of communication, both practically and in how it developed an active professional community. In Figure 2.1, we include a sample e-mail from Liz Lauben, a later chair of the House committee. It provides a taste of Suzy's interaction with the working group leaders. It also demonstrates the coaching emphasis on concrete planning as fundamental to the working groups' functioning, including specifying timelines and roles, as well as making decisions and plans public.

Expanding Structures—and Participation

With the three working groups up and running, and a more trusting relationship established between Suzy and the principal, Nick and Suzy actively looked for ways to expand the organizational development the summer institute planning had initiated. Over the course of their second year working together, their meetings began to take on a more structural focus as they met weekly to support the decisionmaking and planning capacity of the working groups and consider how other aspects of school life could be organized in similar fashion, that is, with faculty input and teacher leadership.

They began by looking at all the meetings and formal groups that existed or could exist. The Cabinet was created in the second year, envisioned as an "ubercommittee" providing vision for and coordination among the other groups. It included people in leadership roles across the school, including the chairs of the three committees, the grade-level coordinators, and the dean (a NYC position that handles student discipline). The Cabinet was responsible for making some policy changes, for example, a cell phone ban (before the DOE adopted a citywide ban) and lateness policy. (While the Cabinet was useful in this regard, it did not achieve the schoolwide leadership and steering function Nick and Suzy originally envisioned.)

Another structure that became increasingly important is the academic departments, which emerged out of the next year's summer institute planning. Nick officially named point people for each department, including John for the social studies department. The departments began meeting monthly and over time increased this to twice a month. Suzy describes the departments' work as largely "task-oriented," focusing on planning courses for the year, rather than "big goal" oriented. The school also created grade-level coordinators, a teacher who is primarily responsible for parent contact and case-conferencing by students' teachers.

Figure 2.1. Sample E-mail

From: [Liz]
Subject: review house minutes . . .
Date: May 6, 2004, 9:33:15 A.M. EDT
To: [Suzy]

Suzy, please review this. I need an introduction and I am at a loss for how to explain what this is . . . is it administrative stuff . . . and then I will send it out. Also, Ed and I devised some flyers and Ed is going to have Van [AP] make a big poster.

Greetings from the House Committee!!

Meeting: Wednesday May 5th, per. 6 in Jeanette's Room

In attendance: Jeanette, Liz, Scott, Suzy, Nick [principal], and Van [AP]

1. **Report card distribution**—Report cards will be distributed in House on Wednesday, May 12. Teachers can pick up their report cards in the main office on the morning of the twelfth. For those students who are not present, please give the report cards back to Yvette.

2. **Intramural prizes** will be given out by Scott in House on June 2. Each of the finalists will receive a $10 gift certificate for Barnes and Nobles and ribbons will be given out to all of the participants.

3. **Attendance**—In order to boost the attendance numbers in the final months of school (April, May, and June), the House committee proposed a "system of rewards" for the house that had the best overall attendance percentage and for those houses that attained 85% attendance. The goal here is 85%. For those houses that achieved the 85%, the students will get a pizza party. Each student in the house with the best attendance percentage will receive a $10 gift certificate to Barnes and Noble. Lynelle has been able to compile a list of the percentages for each house for the month of April. Each teacher will be notified of their percentage and the percentages of the winners. FYI: Drew's house had the best overall attendance for the month of April, so each of his students will receive a gift certificate. Clancy, Jackie and Liz's houses had percentages over 85%, so those students will enjoy a pizza party. Everyone will get their individual percentage number on Monday.

When to expect the "prizes": For planning purposes, the winners can expect to reap the rewards on the *second house meeting* of each month. So, sorry for the short notice . . . but Drew can expect to give out the gift certificates in House on Wednesday, May 12. Clancy, Jackie and Liz can also plan to have pizza in house on the twelfth. (Xiomara [parent coordinator] will order the pizza on Tuesday and Nick will make sure the pizza is distributed to the proper houses on Wednesday.)

(continued)

Figure 2.1. (continued)

What to expect in June: On June 1st, Lynelle will compile a list of percentages for the month of May. Each teacher will be notified of their percentage and the winners by House on Wednesday, June 2. If your house is a winner, please expect to have pizza or hand out gift certificates in the following house, so on JUNE 9. Around the fifteenth of June, another list will be compiled of the attendance numbers for June. (We know it is only about two weeks, but we are hoping that this will motivate some students to stick it out and come to school in June.) Again, teachers will be notified of the numbers sometime during Regents week. If your house is a winner, please plan to have pizza or hand out gift certificates on the last day of school, better known as Close-out day, on June 25th.

Summary of Dates (regarding House):
   May 12—Attendance rewards for the month of April, distribution of report cards
   June 2—Distribution of Intramural prizes
   June 9—Attendance rewards for the month of May
   June 25—Attendance reward for the month of June

4. And lastly, the House committee is preparing for a full staff discussion of House during the 5/18 and 5/25 PD sessions. Thank you for your time in filling out the surveys and for your feedback!!

While all the structures fulfill necessary roles within the school, it is the working groups that have become, according to Suzy, the "backbone of the school." One of Suzy's coaching priorities has been to work with the administration to make the role of working group chair more institutionalized: "They have moral authority but are not compensated for the work they do for the school."

In the coach's mind, at least, the organizational changes had more at stake than just a smoothly running school. Her explicit goal was to create a "professional community in which teachers meet to build the school and problem-solve issues." Toward this end, Suzy continued to meet regularly with a voluntary ISA team, mainly ninth- and tenth-grade teachers, but anyone who was interested about ways to deepen the work related to the ISA principles. One of the key tools Suzy introduced that year to develop that collaborative capacity was protocols.

The Power of Protocol and Other Tools

The notion of using a protocol to structure meetings and professional development sessions was familiar to Suzy from her work at UHHS and relationships with Nancy Mohr, Alan Dichter, David Allen, and other educators who practice them as a form of collaborative professional development. A protocol, in this context, refers to a set of steps for the discussion, for example, presentation, clarifying questions, feedback, and so on, as well as the establishment of roles—presenter, facilitator, participants—and norms for participation.

Suzy saw an opportunity in the second year to introduce protocols as a form of professional development through the work of the Professional Development (PD) Committee, formerly a working group, which was charged with planning weekly whole-faculty professional development sessions. The committee had agreed to emphasize sharing good practices that already existed within the school in order to begin conversations about improving instruction, especially writing instruction, which related to the ISA principle of literacy across the curriculum.

Suzy worried about how to support teachers in sharing their work in a way that would be safe and productive, given the school's lack of experience with faculty collaboration, let alone peer critique.

In Chapter 6, we describe how the PD committee introduced protocols and gradually led the teachers from using protocols to examine work from an external (ISA-provided) writing assessment to presenting their own assignments, tasks, and projects for their colleagues to offer feedback on. By the fifth year of Suzy's coaching relationship with the school, PD sessions incorporated "Slice" protocols (McDonald et al., 2007), in which the faculty was reviewing and discussing work from every teacher's classroom in the school. But at this early stage, it was enough to be able to declare that protocols had arrived at Park East.

The success of protocols in the PD context led Suzy to consider other ways protocols could support the new structure and new emphasis on collaboration. An opportunity to deepen the school's use of protocols came in the summer of 2004 when Alan Dichter, the school's Local Instructional Superintendent, announced a Facilitators' Institute for the schools he worked with. The institute was structured to introduce participants to a range of protocols and provide guidance and practice in facilitating protocols. It also incorporated time to plan for how the protocols could be integrated with the schools' work.

Suzy and six others from Park East participated, including Nick, Van, John Giambalvo, Joe Schmidt, and Liz Lauben. Suzy recalls, "It was a great bonding experience for us. It resulted in a good plan for the beginning of the school year but mostly it left us with a cadre of people who felt comfortable facilitating. This was a tremendous professional experience for us, the learning from which continues to be used throughout the school." The institute resulted in two of the three working group leaders being trained as facilitators, and thus becoming more confident in the role.

Suzy describes one of the outcomes from the institute and follow-up sessions: "Before any event now we routinely talk about how we will do it, the 'pedagogy of a meeting,' in fact—a practice I attribute directly to the Facilitators' Institute." Joe connects skills learned at the Facilitators' Institute with almost every facet of the Park East faculty professional life: "The structure of protocols, the role of the facilitator, the expectation that growth as a community comes from feedback—all of these things the original seven of us learned, and now the school is attuned to their importance as well."

The institute and several follow-up sessions that occurred during the school year, one of which Nick hosted at Park East, encouraged the emergence of a common language of reflection among the administrators and the teacher leaders, as well as cemented the necessity of particular norms for meetings expected by ISA, which Suzy had tried to emphasize from the beginning: having an agenda, designating a point person or facilitator, and establishing norms, or guidelines, for participation.

Another outcome of the institute was Suzy and Nick's decision to apply for a facilitator's endorsement from the National School Reform Faculty's New York center, which required preparing a portfolio that demonstrated how they had used different protocols and reflective pieces about their experiences. "We read each other's drafts and gave each other feedback on the documents," Suzy says, "which turned out to be a great shared experience for the two of us." By this point, as it did with several schools, ISA started to tap Nick and Suzy and others from the school to talk about their progress in a variety of public events. Planning for their presentations and talking publicly about the early progress the school had made solidified Suzy and Nick's relationship and deepened its collaborative nature.

During the second year of Suzy's coaching, an opportunity arose to work with Sandy Abrams, the ISA leadership coach, on an internal "walkthrough" process Sandy was developing to support schools' self-assessment of their instructional practice. Suzy jumped at the chance, bringing the idea of working with Sandy to Nick and the PD Committee as another tool for focusing on instruction across the school. With Sandy's support, the school piloted the walkthroughs that spring and continued with them into the next year, trying various configurations, including within departments and by small groups visiting multiple classes. Joe credits the walkthroughs with being a "watershed" moment at the school. "Now doors were open and we were comfortable with sharing practices." With a new principal and new professional development priorities, formal walkthroughs were not continued; however, the focus on sharing instructional practices endured, as well as the hard-won open-door culture.

By the end of year 3 of Suzy's coaching, the structures for supporting key elements of the school's work were in place, and the faculty-led
groups were developing comfort using protocols and other tools to support collaboration. Looking ahead, Suzy saw her role on the organizational
level less as developing new structures and more as "trying to stretch an
existing group to focus on instructional goals and quality."

Coaching Habits Examined

Coaching habits evident in this stage emphasize developing and expanding structures and introducing and practicing tools for collaboration.

- *Pushing for structures that support collaboration,* including working
  groups (committees), departments, and the Cabinet.
- *Modeling the norms for collaboration,* as indicated in the ISA model, including developing and keeping minutes and posting them publicly.
- *Making connections, sharing strengths* through identifying examples
  of good practice going on within the school, and finding ways to
  share and reflect on these.
- *Using tools* for collaborative sharing and feedback, especially protocols, facilitation training, and the instructional walkthroughs.

STAGE 3—ADDRESSING QUALITY AND RESPONSIVENESS

Our discussion of the third stage of coaching is briefer than the previous
two, since much of the contents of the book focuses on coaching habits
and practices from this stage.

The story of Suzy's coaching and the school's development took
an unexpected turn at the end of the third year when Nick Mazzarella
announced that he would be taking the job of principal at a school in
Brooklyn, and Kevin McCarthy, a first-time principal and new to the
school, took over.

In addition to a new principal, the year started with 10 new teachers. Of
course, this also meant that some of the teachers who had been involved in
the school's transformation so far had left. The school had now established
structures (work groups, Cabinet), norms (use of protocols, giving each other
feedback, doing things openly), and a commitment to instructional improvement. However, the staff turnover necessitated a new emphasis on bringing
more people into the schoolwide work—both faculty members new to the
staff and those who have been on the periphery of the work—and deepening
the quality of the work both organizationally and instructionally.

Suzy saw her role as challenging and supporting the working group leaders and the Cabinet to constantly exercise "responsiveness to the larger group, especially as practices became routine." The change in leadership meant that Suzy would also be working closely with Kevin to articulate his goals for the school and help him understand the roles and responsibilities of the working groups, and consider how these goals would work productively with the existing structures.

Suzy's coaching in this stage emphasized doing the organizational work of the school in a very public, inclusive fashion, and inviting feedback at every step. Suzy encouraged school leaders, now including the leaders of the working groups, now referred to as committees, to make sure to invite new members to join the groups; create opportunities for people to "regroup," that is, switch committees; and reflect on each event. These practices can be seen in action in the Thanksgiving story Alexis tells in Chapter 6; and in Chapter 7, we take a detailed look at how coaching supports the development of teacher leaders as well as works with the principal and other administrators.

On the instructional level, Suzy focused her coaching on working with new teachers. As she had in Stage 1, she worked with the teachers to plan instructional units and projects, as well as the overall curriculum sequence for their courses. In Chapter 4, Jennie's story provides an up-close look at Suzy's planning with a new teacher.

To provide resources for more experienced teachers, and continue the push for quality and depth of instruction, Suzy facilitated new relationships between ISA's literacy and science content coaches and some of those teachers she had worked with in the past. For example, Joe began to meet regularly with Phyllis Tashlik, the ISA literacy content coach, on new projects related to *Huckleberry Finn* and *The Tempest*, and Liz Lauben, a science teacher Suzy had worked with the previous year, began to work with Marc Siciliano, the ISA science content coach, on reorganizing an introductory-level science course to focus on human impact.

The focus on instructional planning evident in the previous stages had resulted in significant changes from the school we described in Stage 1. Now there are examples across the curriculum of students reading real books, especially in English and social studies classes; writing assignments scaffold students' progress through the writing process; and many more multistep projects culminate in a product. In addition, as Suzy describes, "College expectations are in the air. There are fewer repeater classes, more attention to failing students, and the rate of college-going has increased, and test scores are solid in all disciplines." Alexis points to the development of elective courses for seniors, along with the reduction in the need for repeater courses, and an increase in the number of students who pass the Regents on their first attempt, as the biggest changes in the school's instructional climate. And by the DOE's measures, Park East is off of the SINI list (schools in need of improvement) and earned a grade B on its last school report card.

Planning with teachers on the instructional level and with school leaders on the organizational level have remained central to Suzy's work as a coach; however, in this stage, the nature of her involvement has shifted somewhat from active co-planner to helpful "nudge" or "encourager." One of the coaching habits that remains constant from the first days through the changes in role we have described has been to communicate her enthusiasm for the little steps and signs of progress made by individuals and groups in the school—more about this in the following chapters.

Coaching Habits Examined

Coaching habits evident in this stage reflect Suzy's stepping back to allow established and emerging leaders room to lead:

- *Resourcing*: Connecting teachers to instructional resources, such as the ISA content coaches.
- *Expanding inclusion* to a greater part of the faculty, especially new teachers.
- *Checking in* regularly with established leaders and developing leaders to see what kinds of support they need.
- *Sharing enthusiasm!*

CHAPTER 3

Organizing
Coaching Time

Many if not all coaches struggle with the problem of how they can do everything they need to do, speak with everybody they need to speak with, make notes on everything they need to make notes on, and so on. The answer is, of course, they can't. Coaching is an impossible job, the way good teaching is an impossible job or being a good principal is an impossible job. The only way we know to approach an impossible job that will yield actual results is to plan very carefully how those precious hours, days, and weeks will be spent; always be open to changing the plan in response to what occurs in the actual moment; and continually reflect on how the plan is meeting immediate needs and longer-term goals.

In the previous chapter, we provided some historical context for coaching at Park East High School by describing how the coaching and the school have developed over a period of 5 years. In this chapter, we are also concerned with time, but in smaller units: weeks, days, and hours.

In the remainder of the chapter, Suzy describes how she thinks about and organizes her time in the school, and some of it outside the school. Throughout, we call out some of the key coaching habits and practices that are evident at different points in the work.

WEEKLY ROUTINES IN AND OUT
OF SCHOOL (SUZY)

Park East High School, like a lot of schools, can be a chaotic place. In order to make the most of my limited time in the school, not to mention stay relatively sane, I have established a few core rituals. In this section, I describe five: 1) the Sunday e-mail; 2) the "hit list"; 3) the mobile office; 4) logging and journaling; and 5) hitting "REPLY."

Sunday E-mail

For the past 2 years, since Nick (the principal) asked me to expand my coaching from one day to two, I have been at the school for 2 days a week, typically Tuesday and Wednesday. However, my work week at Park East always starts with the Sunday-night e-mail. I usually sit down around 7:00 P.M. to type up my schedule for the week in preparation for posting on the faculty listserv (see Chapter 2). I always think carefully about the time I send it—not too early on Sunday, if possible, so as not to bust into people's weekends; but also not too late, so that they get it before Monday morning when they are quickly already deep into the week's hubbub.

I started sending out the weekly e-mail as a way to practice open communication about my activities back in the days when secrecy was the prevailing "MO" at Park East. As we described in Chapter 2, there was a time when there was almost no public communication about professional responsibilities and no sharing of information regarding the various meetings that took place at the school. People worked in vacuums and protected their territory. I saw my weekly e-mail posted on the listserv as a small challenge to that.

> *Coaching Habit:*
> ▶ *Communicating regularly and openly*, for example, by making plans and schedules explicit in writing and sending them out publicly

Though the public nature of my e-mail is, thankfully, no longer needed as a way to buck the status quo, in addition to the obvious direct purpose of letting people know where I am, what I will be doing, and who I expect to meet with me, it is a ritual I continue to practice largely because of the tone of organization and planning I hope to communicate in all I do. To me, it speaks in a small way to my big commitment to openness, collaboration, and follow-through. In Figure 3.1, I give an example of a typical weekly e-mail.

Weekly "Hit List"

In addition to the Sunday e-mail of my schedule that goes out to the entire faculty via the listserv, each week I make a "hit list," as in what I need to remember to "hit" or do at school and what I plan to discuss with each individual or group I meet with. So that the list is easy to put my hands on when I need to refer to it, I write it onto a brightly colored piece of paper

Figure 3.1. Sample Weekly E-mail

From: [SUZY]
Subject: [PEHS] schedule for week of 10/16
Date: October 15, 2006, 8:08:33 P.M. EDT
To: [PEHS-STAFF]
Reply-To: [PEHS-STAFF]

Hi Everyone,

Here's my plan for Tues and Wed. Please email me any changes (off listserv). Diky (that's Czech for—)

Tues
PD   [Faculty professional development session]
pd 1   Clancy
pd 2   Diedre
pd 3   Joe/Jennie
pd 4   Jean Claude
pd 5   Kevin and Karen
pd 6   Nicole if Chris can switch (otherwise, Nicole can you do 4th on Wed?)
pd 7   Peter
pd 8   Chris and Marc
SLC mtg after school

Wed
pd 1   Carrie
pd 2   Brianne
pd 4   Nicole if not Tues
pd 5   Alexis
pd 6   Paul
pd 7   Nikki
pd 8   House committee—reviewing process for progress reports—any thoughts faculty have on the idea in general and the process in specific please let us know or join us for the meeting if you can. We will also talk re the Nov calendar for House.

FYI: Thursday
pd 6   Pine Manor, a girls college outside Boston where we have a PE alum in attendance, is sending us a rep to talk to our students—senior girls invited to attend. Talk to Jeannette or Jean Claude if you have recommendations.

Thanks.

Suzy

---

that I clip in as the first page of what people jokingly refer to as my "mobile office," in other words, the three-ring binder that goes everywhere and does everything with me while I am at Park East.

> ***Coaching Habit:***
> ► *Nailing down the details,* for example, by keeping all important materials handy and specifying concrete plans and goals for upcoming meetings.

Throughout the day, I continuously consult the hit list and the thoughts included therein, as well as other resources in my binder such as the school's master schedule, the bell schedule, the yearly calendar, marking period dates, and so on (see Figure 3.2). For ease of reference, I divide the weekly hit list into sections. The righthand side includes my schedule, period by period, for each of the two days, along with small notes by the names of each individual regarding issues I plan to discuss with them. The lefthand side and most of the center of the page is a general to-do list and includes items such as "Prepare ISA student surveys for distribution." The bottom half of the page is reserved for recording agenda items for my meetings with the assistant principal and the principal as well as each of the three committee meetings plus the Cabinet that I attend regularly.

I will often stick Post-its onto the hit list with questions I want to ask specific people or ideas I want to share. I also use these for last-minute things I think of that need to get done.

The plans for what I want to talk to people about are usually very specific and concrete, like "February calendar for the House Committee," or "Graphic organizers for Liz" because she asked me for examples. As things occur to me over the course of the time I am away from Park East, I write them down on the "overall" part of the colored piece of paper; for example, I might write, "Check with Kevin [the principal] re historical figure graphic books for Carrie [ESL teacher]," because I had heard Kevin or Karen (a pseudonym), a new AP, say they might be too expensive to order. Before I start planning curriculum with Carrie around these books, I will make sure that we can get them.

Mobile Office

Whenever possible, I meet with teachers in their own rooms, in order for teachers to have their materials handy as we plan and to know something about their classroom. This means that much of my day is spent going from classroom to classroom, and while I do have a home base at Park East—I share the social studies office—I am most often on the move.

Figure 3.2. Sample Weekly "Hit List"

Park East March 13, 14

- **talk to John A re coaching volleyball**
- **Chris and Joe – coaching per session to ISA**
- **Brady – PE Slamz PO to ISA**

Kevin and Karen
- trophy ordering
- paying for Pinewood Manor
- extended day grant
- 2nd round of admissions
- set up programming meeting

House committee
- go over feedback from last session
- plan next week's session

Tuesday
PD – dept meetings (ask English dept for list of books read)
Pd 1 PD mtg
Pd 2 Joe's class (ask re helping with intramurals)
Pd 3 observe different classes
Pd 4 Alexis (ask re anatomy lab manuals)
Pd 5 Kevin and Karen
Pd 6 Jennie
Pd 7 coaches mtg
Pd 8 Liz's class (ask re dissection club)

Wednesday
Extended day – Linda re getting ready for Regents
Pd 2 Brianne (re tech club, writing project)
Pd 3 prep for House
House
Pd 5 House committee meeting
Pd 6 Diedre's class
Pd 7 Chris (re donors choose, model student bulletin board, athletic banquet)
Pd 8 Marcia (re college going lists)
Cabinet

Early on I started carrying a notebook and a binder to keep notes from my meetings with and observations of teachers as well as any lessons, assignments, or samples of student work I had collected. I also developed the practice of holding onto lists, schedules, calendars, and organizational tools that were once tightly held by their creators. I started carrying these around to different meetings so as to promote collaboration and to keep them handy if a question arose, for instance, when to plan for a particular event or which teacher might be free during a given period in order to set up a peer observation.

The practice of taking notes, saving materials created or used by teachers, as well as student work samples, and having them handy when needed, in my mind, contributes to overall organization as well as promotes collaboration and professional community through the sharing of resources. Collecting and sharing artifacts also concretizes the work and helps us to build on what we have done already, be it teachers' lesson plans or plans for a professional development day. When we go back to old work before planning new experiences, the result can be more efficient as well as richer and deeper.

Coaching Habit:

▶ *Writing it down*: documenting through taking notes and saving artifacts, such as schedules, calendars, samples of teachers' assignments and student work, etc.

Logging and Journaling

After my last day at Park East for the week I usually close out the week by logging what I have actually done (versus what I had intended to do) in the last section of my three-ring binder. In my log I record brief details about the outcomes of my meetings, such as "planned field trip to Central Park with Paul [science teacher]" or "honed paper topic with Joe."

I started logging to facilitate writing invoices for ISA but I have found that logging actually helps me keep track of outcomes as well as identify patterns of change. It is where I notice that I have missed a meeting with someone for a couple of weeks in a row. Or if I do not have much to write in terms of "outcomes," I think about whether that is because we worked on so many different things that it is hard to record briefly or because we "just talked" and did not, in fact, get much done. I use logging as another means to help me think about what I do and how I might do it better. But primarily, the purpose of the log in my mind is to record on a pretty basic level when and with whom I have met.

After logging, I reflect in my on-the-computer Park East journal. The journal is informal and meant for me—no complete sentences allowed! Entries are sometimes venting, sometimes goal-setting, sometimes planning new strategies, but always a way of processing the week. In the journal I try to sketch out dilemmas I am having or thoughts about new projects or resources people might be interested in. I write about different ways I might be able to further the work. Rarely do I read old entries,

ideas about journaling

unless I am writing an end-of-the-year/-semester report or reflection. Mostly I use the journal as a routine, which serves as an outlet through which to air frustration and, conversely, to record successes so they do not just evaporate.

Coaching Habit:
▶ Reflecting systematically through keeping logs and journals

After I journal, I take out my colored piece of paper and begin composing my weekly hit list again, starting with the overall things I want to get done in the coming week and then planning for each of my individual meetings with teachers, administrators, and our committees.

Hitting "REPLY"

A good portion of my coaching work happens on days when I am not at Park East but am still available to teachers and administrators via e-mail. I consider e-mail communication (and less frequently the phone) a natural outgrowth of our meeting time: at the table we make plans, then teachers go home and actually write something for distribution to students or a lesson for a class, at which point they are ready for more specific feedback. Over e-mail teachers sometimes send assignments for me to look over. Most of the time they make quick requests for resources such as the following e-mail from Jackie, an English teacher:

> I hope you had a nice weekend. I was just planning for the week and I was wondering if you thought of any Oedipus movie that I can show my senior class.
>
> Thanks,
Jackie

Other times they are more elaborate. For example, Brianne, a social studies teacher, wrote:

> Hi Suzy,
> My kids are starting their projects tomorrow and I'd like to do an exercise relating to how to caption the pictures they find. I want them to write good captions but I'm not exactly sure what I'm looking for or how to model it. I was thinking of giving them some sentence starters and some sample pictures to work with as a Do Now on Thursday . . . any ideas??? See you Thursday!
>
> Brianne

Here is my reply to Brianne:

> I think always a good place to start is giving them some captions and photos and asking what do they notice about what makes a good caption (maybe like 3 things such as: tells what's in the picture, gives a bit of interesting info about what's in the pictures, points out something you might not notice like a symbol, includes a date, etc. . . .). And then have them practice individually as part of your Do Now and then go over as a class a couple of different kinds (i.e.: interesting info vs. just says what's there). The single biggest thing I'd point out is that their captions should never start with "This is. . . . " Any of those immediately hit the circular file. . . . Cut to the chase, interesting language, interesting info that tells about the picture is where it's at.
>
> Check in with Jackie too. She did a nice caption project when she read *Night* last year.
>
> Hope this helps.
>
> Suzy

Coaching Habits:
- ▶ *Checking in* with teachers (and administrators) through regular, informal communication
- ▶ *Offering feedback* on teachers' lesson plans and other documents they create (often through e-mail)
- ▶ *Making connections, sharing strengths* through encouraging one teacher (Brianne) to check in with another (Jackie) who has done something similar that could serve as a resource or model. This also relates to the coaching habit of *recycling* materials

Gathering Resources

Another aspect of my coaching work that happens largely away from school is resource-gathering. I am always on the lookout for books, materials, movies, field trip sites, and ideas that a teacher I am working with can use. Never mind the years teaching or the doctorate in education, I often claim that reading the *New York Times* is the wellspring of my coaching career—a joke, but not entirely . . .

Teachers sometimes ask me for specific resources that I try to hunt down. I also pass a lot of materials on to them from my own teaching practice, from ISA coaches' meetings, or from other teachers at schools I have known and visited. Reading an article in the *Times* and bringing it to a teacher represents to me a potential source of information and inspiration.

It also signals, I hope, to the teachers that I think about their classes and what they do on my own time as well. It is a way through which I communicate my enthusiasm and support for their work as well.

Reading professionally and widely, outside of the profession but in the areas related to what I do and think about at Park East, and bringing those readings back to the school is one of the most critical elements of my coaching work.

Coaching Habits:
▶ *Resourcing*: gathering and sharing resources related to classes taught or interests of teacher and sharing with teachers
▶ *Making connections, sharing strengths* through matching people who can be resources, within the school or outside of it, with people who could benefit
▶ *Sharing enthusiasm* by letting teachers know the coach is thinking about their classes and plans, and keeping an eye out for resources that might help them.

Resources to me are both material and human. A part of any coaching week for me involves leveraging the human resources at ISA as well as within Park East. I spend a period of time each week coordinating, mostly via e-mail, the visits of ISA subject specialty coaches like Phyllis Tashlik (literacy) and Marc Siciliano (science) to Park East.

DECIDING HOW TO SPEND MY TIME (SUZY)

The Sunday e-mail encapsulates the decisions I make regarding the use of my time. Essentially I divide my time at Park East into three distinct categories:

- Teacher time (usually with individuals, sometimes with pairs; in meetings, in class, or at "events" organized by a particular teacher).
- Committee meetings (Professional Development Committee, the House Committee, the Student Life Committee, Cabinet, etc.).
- Weekly meetings with the principal and AP.

Because it is such a limited resource, how I decide to use my time is one of the most important decisions I make in my practice as a coach. I find myself constantly reevaluating my use of time as well as thinking of new ways to maximize it. Because of the reactive, fast-paced culture of most schools, scheduling appointments with individuals and for committee meetings is absolutely essential to avoid getting caught up in the frenzy.

At the same time, flexibility is important, too. I find that once people understand (and experience) that you are there to meet with them during the time you have settled on as mutually convenient, they will forgive (as will you) the times when you have to rearrange the schedule to accommodate a visitor or special observation of a class, etc.

No matter how organized I try to be about time management, due to the frenzied nature of schools and the limited time I have at Park East, I often feel that my work as a coach happens on borrowed time. Routinely it feels that there is not enough time to do all that needs to be done, to accomplish as much as could or should be accomplished. Part of that stems from my own high expectations and part of it from the reality of only having 2 days per week at the school (I often wonder what it would be like to be there more and how dailyness would change the nature of the work).

As it is, because I am only there 2 days per week (albeit in e-mail and phone contact more), I feel an enormous responsibility to use my time well and I quickly make adjustments if something falls through. For example, if a teacher gets a coverage (of a class for a teacher who is absent) during our meeting time and I find myself with an extra period on hand, I will often make brief, unscheduled visits to classes that I do not get to see as much as others.

Sometimes I will take the opportunity to pop my head into all classrooms going on during that period—a practice I call a sweep. Or else I will check in with some of the people with whom I do not have a regularly scheduled meeting time, such as our school social worker, with whom I like to connect and get his read on the feel of the place, particularly as it relates to faculty morale and overall school climate.

Coaching Habit:
▶ *Being flexible*: adjusting schedule as necessary and having backup activities for when things get rescheduled, such as an informal check-ins or sweeps

At the same time, I have learned that while time is precious, I cannot afford to be too precious about the amount of time I have to work with people. Teachers meet with me during their prep periods, often stuck in between two classes. Thus, I feel a tremendous responsibility to not waste their time, to make our meetings useful to them, and to end with a feeling of accomplishment. To achieve this, I have learned to adjust my expectations and work fast and on the fly as well as over somewhat more relaxed time in regular weekly meetings and, when scheduling permits, for longer blocks of time, such as during finals or Regents examinations week (when regular classes do not meet). Yet I have come to see that the quick feedback on a lesson or assignment can be very useful, too, especially if it is part of my repertoire of coaching techniques—sometimes fast, sometimes slow and careful.

WITH WHOM AND DOING WHAT? (SUZY)

Currently I meet regularly with 15 different people—12 teachers, the college advisor, the assistant principal, and the principal—and four configurations (committees) on a regular basis. The way I see it, I have 18 "opportunities" to meet over my 2 days—eight periods per day for the two I am there as well as two afternoons after school. There are 26 teachers on the faculty. Park East has a literacy coach from the Department of Education, a long-time special education teacher at the school who now works as a half-time coach and a half-time transition teacher ("transition" is a course for special ed kids' transition to life after high school). We also have a Department of Education math coach.

Since we were covered in math and English, after my first year at the school, when I worked with all the teachers on the ninth-grade team, Nick Mazzarella, then the principal of Park East, asked me to work primarily with the social studies and science teachers, which I have continued to do with the support of a new principal, Kevin McCarthy. ISA asks coaches to focus coaching work on the core subject areas, so I usually start there and branch out. I have essentially taken the directive from ISA in combination with my assignment from Nick and then Kevin to work with the science and social studies departments to mean that I must work with all the teachers in those departments and then stretch to accommodate others as needed, desired, or requested.

In terms of deciding who to work with I usually put out an e-mail at the beginning of the semester letting people know I am setting up my schedule and requesting them to write in if they would like to arrange a time to meet. My general rule has been to make time for people who ask to see me, even if they are not teachers in the core disciplines or those in the two departments to which I have been assigned. If someone asks for time, I will make every effort to meet the need and negotiate the various internal politics as necessary to do so.

During the 2005–06 school year when Park East had a new principal as well as 10 out of 26 new teachers, I made it a point to meet with all of the new teachers, if some (social studies and science teachers) more regularly than others. At a school with turnover as great as ours, I think that part of the work will always involve helping first-year teachers acculturate to the school and, as much as possible, as we say, "avoid a bomb and survive with aplomb."

Coaching Habit:
▶ *Balancing priorities* through being clear about goals and needs, and "doing the math" to figure out how much time I can spend with different people and groups

In addition to departmental delineations for coaching responsibilities and a commitment to new teachers, level of interest in coaching by a teacher plays a role in my decisions about who to work with. I try hard to meet not only with the people who naturally gravitate to such opportunities. I consider it part of the practice of coaching to go after the resisters, the less gung-ho, those who, frankly, do not necessarily want to be coached. And so I interpret—or leverage—the charge of meeting with the social studies and science departments as a way to set up appointments with all teachers in those departments regardless of their level of interest.

Coaching Habit:
▶ *Looking for entry points/levers for change*, for example, by turning required meetings into opportunities for building relationships and collaboration

Lately I have been feeling that the time I have to meet with people is too limited and that the one-on-one meeting method is too time consuming and rather—I am loath to use this word—inefficient. And so I have been trying to figure out how to organize my time to meet with groups of people, by department or common interest. But no good answer has emerged so far and remains something I continue to work on.

The irony of this work is that though I strive to be unbelievably planful about how my time is spent, often the most powerful moments are those that happen on the fly, the "drive-by handoff"—for example, passing an example of a strong assignment or piece of student work from one teacher to another in the hallway on the way to class (see Chapter 5 for the story of "traveling BBQ"). Making connections among people in the hallways, remembering who did what and who needs to ask who for what as we pass on the way to class; all these things matter.

The key to seeing growth is in the short, unplanned moments because they reflect the strength of the professional community; in what's taken for granted it is possible to see how far we've come. Ironically, perhaps, it is the intense planning I do that helps make them possible.

CHAPTER 4

Planning for Instruction

Planning is at the center of school coaching; it grounds and unifies nearly everything the coach does. As Joe observed in an interview:

> I think the one thing [about Suzy's coaching] that absolutely jumps out in my mind is her use of and focus on the importance of planning. Things need to be planned, preplanned. We need to sit down and have meetings, meetings before the meetings, agendas, that are all around planning. I think that's the number one thing that Suzy does over and over.

Examining Suzy's coaching practice yields multiple examples of planning: in how she plans her own week and day, as described in Chapter 3; in regular meetings with individual teachers or pairs of teachers to plan curriculum and instruction; in meetings with committee chairs to go over the agenda for an upcoming event or professional development session; and in working with the principal and other school leaders to address schoolwide issues. In addition, there are countless on-the-fly planning sessions that occur during hurried in-between-classes discussions, what Joe McDonald (1989) calls "three-legged conversations"; quick check-ins with teachers during a free period; and e-mails and phone calls that might involve planning a class assignment or firming up a committee agenda.

As she described in Chapter 3, collaborative planning of instruction with teachers makes up the biggest chunk of Suzy's time at Park East: "By planning, I mean working with a teacher to develop a lesson or classroom activity, project or assignment. This could be poring over a book and figuring out how to introduce it to students or spending forty-five minutes hammering out a good question to ask in a final paper."

To explore this crucial component of coaching, this chapter presents three stories told by teachers, each with a unique scope, in terms of the coaching relationship, and focus, in terms of curriculum and instruction. Figure 4.1 provides an overview of the three stories.

Figure 4.1. Overview of Planning Stories

Title	Scope and Theme	Author
Planning "Our Water" Project	Working with a teacher initially resistant to coaching; planning a longer-term student project.	Alexis
Bringing in the Books	Working with a new teacher; incorporating authentic texts into curriculum.	Jennie
Teaching Writing Transformed	Working with a teacher over time; developing effective writing prompts and assessments.	Joe

Each story is followed by a reflection on how it surfaces some key coaching habits, which we call out within the stories, related to instructional planning. Individually, the stories can function as case studies to explore coaching habits and practices that support teachers in developing their repertoire of instructional practices—and their own capacity to plan instruction. In the Chapter 5, we address some coaching practices that relate strongly to planning, including observation, providing resources, fostering connections, and checking in with teachers.

PLANNING "OUR WATER" PROJECT (ALEXIS)

Alexis is a fifth-year science teacher at Park East, one of just three teachers in that department. She began working with Suzy when she became head of the Student Life committee. Only in the last two years has she begun to work with Suzy on her classroom instructional planning, a gradual "chipping-away" process Alexis describes below.

I will be the first to admit I have always been wary of working with Suzy to discuss planning for two very different reasons. First, I was not a part of the initial group Suzy had sought out to work with and I was resentful of that—I was just a first-year teacher during her first year at Park East and I felt there was a clear separation between those on the "team" and those not. The second reason was time; when Suzy did want to work with me I felt like it was a commitment I was not sure I had the time for.

I have slowly come around to seeing the value in my meeting time with Suzy (especially in a semester in which I have the pleasure of three preps). Suzy is extremely good at locating the small hole in the wall to begin to chip away at. Our working relationship started with the Student Life committee. She then saw my interest in pursuing an anatomy elective and used that to help inform my practice. She worked hard to help me get the elective offered and begin the planning stages. I may tease her about her methods of nagging or chipping away, but I value her persistence, as it has greatly helped my development of both a course I really enjoy teaching and also one that I had no idea how to proceed with.

"Our Water"

In trying to teach the water cycle to a group of uninterested ninth graders I veered off topic and tried to grasp their attention by talking about the waste water cycle. As I described what happens to their goldfish when it gets flushed down the toilet, a student spoke up and asked if we could watch a movie about what happens to water. I mistakenly took that to mean a movie on the water cycle and soon after I showed them a film about evaporation, cloud formation, and precipitation. When the film was over, she was angry because she meant that she wanted to see something about "*our* water." This was when it dawned on me that she wanted to see what happened to sewage.

I realized this could be a great topic to cover during the Human Impact section of our ninth-grade curriculum, and also maybe avoid Suzy's desire to have me incorporate a science fair into my curriculum, something she'd been pushing for months and I'd resisted because I really did not want to add a project that would inevitably be a huge time commitment to my already full plate. As awful as it sounds, I worry about spending too much time on a project of that magnitude that translates to a minuscule portion of the Living Environment Regents, the New York State–required curriculum.

At my next meeting with Suzy, I told her about the idea of maybe taking the students to the sewage treatment plant and spending a good chunk of time on water treatment. She was excited that the idea had been student inspired and was quick to jump on board and help with the planning of this new unit. This is how we decided that an experiment on the drinking water at our school would be a great project for us to do.

At our next meeting, Suzy and I came up with two questions for the students to investigate: "What's better to drink: bottled water or Park East school water?" and "Where in the school is the best water?" We decided that these questions would have a direct impact on the students' lives, considering that they love to complain about the water fountains and how that water is "gross." Since we would be conducting the experiment during the Human Impact section of the curriculum, these guiding questions would allow for some real-world experience to drive their learning experience.

Immediately, we started looking through catalogs for kits to test the water and continued to plan out which places in the building would be interesting to test. Over the course of our next several meetings we ordered the kit, identified a significant list of places to test, and began discussing how to organize the project.

Coaching Habits:
▶ Pushing for student products
▶ Framing questions
▶ Sharing enthusiasm

I decided it would be best if we started the project after the February vacation. This allowed time for developing concepts, including pollution and the impact of humans on the environment. We thought about what the students might need to have reinforced before we started the experiment, specifically which data to collect, how to collect it, and the importance of more than one trial. We also discussed how to tie into the experiment a trip to the sewage treatment plant and how to relate the students' investigations to what they would see when going to the plant.

At our next meeting Suzy presented me with a packet of materials she had gotten from the Department of Environmental Protection (DEP) Web site. We both got really excited as we went through the information and found that there are several prominent city agencies that are out of compliance on their waste water. This led to the idea that if we had the students test the water and we found any place within our building that was out of compliance, we could have the students start a letter-writing campaign. We also found out how completely difficult it is to get in touch with anyone at the DEP or the waste water treatment plant.

While on hold with several different agencies, we laid out a rough map of how to start the project, how many groups to have, and which tests from the test kit we would use. The students would be broken into four groups and would first develop two separate hypotheses based on the two guiding questions and then perform tests that measured the pH, alkalinity, hardness, sulfite, iron, and chloride content of their water. Each day we went to the lab, each group would do several trials for two of the different tests. We also decided that each group would be testing a different floor of the school and different type of bottled water and then comparing it to their classmates' data before drawing any conclusions. I would need to explain the pH scale to the students and briefly discuss what the presence of each of the chemicals would mean for the purity of their water.

We left this meeting with a fairly good idea of when and how I should start the project, and we agreed that we would talk more over break about it and meet again early in the week after break to flesh out more of the project. Of course, not to my surprise, during the break Suzy sent me an FYI e-mail of an article in the paper on the sources of New York's drinking water; but that is just Suzy, always looking for the little things that will make a teacher's life just a little bit easier. Suzy also informed me that she finally got in touch with someone at the waste water plant and they told her they no longer did tours because of security issues. We were both disappointed that this part of the plan would not come to fruition. However, another colleague had a contact at the plant and they sent us a DVD about how waste water is treated, which would at least meet that student's original request to see a movie about "our water."

Coaching Habits:
▶ Outlining the course/project
▶ Resourcing

As the project progressed, the students really got into testing the school's water, but it took longer than we anticipated. It also took a lot more chemicals than it probably should have because of the students' enthusiasm for testing. I started to panic because I was not sure how we would finish if all the groups did a second set of tests on bottled water. I was panicking because of the time constraints but more so because I didn't think we would be able to finish up with the chemicals we had left. I was also starting to wonder where to go instructionally after water treatment finished. At one of my next meetings with Suzy, she suggested that we try to order another kit before altering the original plan. So I sat down with Van, our assistant principal, and tried to find a similar water treatment kit. I was pretty excited when we found one and ordered it right away. While waiting for the next supply to arrive, I needed to fill some space, i.e., class time, with relevant material—it's a good thing I saved the article Suzy had sent me over break. I was able to look at the article with her and develop some questions related to the article, which happened to be about where New York City's drinking water supply came from.

I also looked into the DEP packet Suzy had found and decided to use the water usage worksheets included in it. I told Suzy that I was going to have the students record their water usage, and she could not wait to see the results. We both realized this was not exactly related to what is in the water, but it was definitely pertinent to their lives. When the students finished tracking how much water they used in a week, they were shocked at how many gallons they used a day. Students do not appreciate the finite limit of the resources they take advantage of, and since the major theme for this semester is human impact, I felt justified covering this topic in the midst of waiting for our replacement kit.

Unfortunately, when the kit finally arrived, it was nothing like the first kit, but thankfully Suzy was in school that day and I took the opportunity to brainstorm a plan of action for the second half of this huge project. We sat down and discussed how the students could still test bottled water, yet be conservative with our dwindling chemical supply. Suzy came up with a round-robin approach to testing the water and reducing the numbers of types of bottled water from four to two (we had finished testing the tap water). The students would still have the benefit of multiple trials, but each group would be performing one trial for each of the six tests. The groups would rotate through the tests with each group doing a total of 12 tests (6 for each bottled water type). The four groups would then present their data to one another, and therefore the data tables would include four trials. After we worked out this detail Suzy wanted me to consider having the students put poster boards together to present their findings. I told her that I would consider it after they compiled all the data and wrote up a formal lab report. I gave the students an outline that was to guide them in their lab write-up and I allowed them 4 days of class time to complete much of the lab report.

Coaching Habit:
▶ Problem-solving

After several weeks and a few mini-meltdowns, the students had completed the project and many of them turned in a typed formal lab report. As I started reading the conclusions of some of the students I was disappointed to realize that they made their conclusions with little connection to the data or only used the data that supported their hypotheses. They obviously needed more scaffolding that would help them to really draw valid conclusions from their data. Finding meaningful ways to scaffold the making conclusions portion of an experiment is an aspect Suzy and I really did not spend much time discussing, and it clearly showed in the results.

Nearing the end of the project, I expressed to Suzy that I was not sure how to progress to the other Human Impact topics. This would become the focus of our next several meetings. I also thought that the lab report would be the culmination of the water treatment unit, but thanks to Suzy's always active thought process, I was wrong. Suzy had found another article on prescription medication as an environmental contaminant, which she envisioned me using as an extra-credit project. I used the article to discuss the value of further investigation and the ongoing process of scientific research. I decided it would be a great way to teach the students that even though we had tested the water for several different contaminants, a major part of the scientific process was further investigation.

Coaching Habits Examined

Alexis's story introduces some of the most important and most commonly occurring of the coaching habits Suzy manifests. Many of these habits and practices will show up again in the stories to follow, as well as in the chapters that follow.

Outlining the Course/Project. In one brief paragraph, Alexis provides us a glimpse of how Suzy works with teachers to create an overall schedule for how a project will play out over time, which involved determining which concepts and skills should be reinforced before getting into the water study, which data would be collected and how students would do it, and how to incorporate the (envisioned) visit to the sewage treatment plant into the project.

Suzy comments on some of the benefits of explicitly outlining a project as part of planning:

> Simply put, if you plan for it, it may happen; if you don't, it won't. While some of the elements are likely to change, beginning with an outline allows the teacher to think ahead and make sure all the important big ideas find their way into the plan. It also helps move beyond the "what-am-I-doing-tomorrow?" kind of teaching to more planful and directed instruction that is based on carefully chosen ideas and concepts that are pursued deeply over time. Well-planned assignments that are written down also make teaching easier and better over the long haul because teachers can repeat and deepen rather than continually start from scratch.

Framing Questions. Suzy's coaching does not have an explicit focus on inquiry, but an important aspect of much of her planning with teachers is helping them to frame questions students will address that are important to the discipline and will stimulate student thinking. In Alexis's story, we see how the questions the coach and teacher co-developed, "What's better to drink, bottled water or Park East school water?" and "Where in the school is the best water?" did just that.

Resourcing. Planning involves material resources as well as ideas, questions, and structures. In Alexis's story we see a number of examples of how Suzy helps teachers identify and obtain resources, from poring over catalogs for water testing kits to checking out the DEP Web site for possible data and keeping her eye out for articles that could enrich the project—or, as Alexis notes, help fill unexpected classroom space (time).

Pushing for Student Products. Early in Alexis's story, she mentions that Suzy had been urging her to consider a science fair as a way to incorporate student products into the curriculum. While Alexis resisted that idea, Suzy did not give up on the idea of student products. When the idea of studying sewage treatment occurred to Alexis, Suzy seized it as another opportunity to incorporate a longer-term student research project into the curriculum. Later in Alexis's story, we hear about Suzy's suggestion that students create poster boards to present their findings from the water testing.

Incorporating significant student product not only serves as a capstone to the project, according to Suzy, it also

> recognizes the students as completing something relevant and meaningful, with real-life application. It also serves as a kind of public service announcement by getting the word out to the rest of the school—a quiet message that schoolwork can be deeply meaningful and important in and to the world. We are always making this case to our students, helping them to connect to their work, and feel pride and ownership in it; products and especially the public display of these products aids this process.

Problem-Solving. Even when it is well-planned, problems are likely to arise during the course of any complex, long-term project. Suzy's view of coaching and teaching as problem-solving is evident in the way she works with Alexis to turn obstacles into learning opportunities, for example, when she helped Alexis figure out a system that would allow all of the students to complete multiple water tests with dwindling resources and time.

Sharing Enthusiasm. As Suzy supports teachers to step outside their comfort zones with projects like the "Our Water" study, she recognizes the need for intellectual, material, and moral support. One of the most striking aspects of Suzy's coaching is her blend of practical problem-solving and enthusiastic encouragement for teachers. It is perhaps because of her familiarity with how challenging the conditions are for good teaching that she is so enthusiastic about the small breakthroughs that teachers make as they stretch out of their comfort zones, for example, her response to Alexis's idea of having students record their own water use.

BRINGING IN THE BOOKS (JENNIE)

Jennie was in her first year as a full-time social studies teacher when she started working with Suzy. In the story she relates below, she describes how Suzy worked with her on introducing a "real" book, as opposed to textbook readings, into her curriculum, something she had never done before. The idea of using real books, rather than just textbooks, in classes across the curriculum was one of Suzy's coaching goals, and consistent with the ISA instructional focus on literacy across the curriculum. As Jennie describes, she, like Alexis, initially had her doubts about working with a coach.

I began as a first-year teacher at Park East in the fall of 2005, and as a part of the social studies department, Suzy became my coach. Although I agreed to meet with her and another first-year Global Studies teacher on a weekly basis, I felt resistant to any type of help or guidance. After completing what I thought was a rigorous student teaching program and graduating from Pennsylvania State University, I thought I was very well prepared for any teaching experience. Suzy approached us to find which common prep period we had in order to meet. I did not feel like this was an optional meeting, so I decided to "play along," but, in my defiance, I felt like I had little to learn, so I took these meetings lightly. Shortly into the school year, especially when I began to feel the stresses of a first-year teacher, I learned how valuable these meetings would become to my instructional practice.

A New Course

During the spring semester of my first year, I was scheduled to teach an economics course to juniors and seniors. I felt anxious about teaching this course, since economics was my weakest subject within the social studies discipline, and so I had initial feelings of incompetence. Before the semester began, Suzy sat down with me to outline the course, alleviating some of my worries. It was during this time that she suggested I incorporate a book into the curriculum. It would not only be a relatively easy way for me to teach economics—since I had no text or solid curriculum with which to work, a book seemed liked a sound base from which to build—but would be beneficial for our students, who had read few full books throughout their high school experiences.

Suzy had a few ideas of books I could use. I read some of them to find one that I thought would be most interesting and chose Barbara Ehrenreich's *Nickel and Dimed* (2001), one that Suzy most strongly advocated.

Coaching Habits:
- ▶ Outlining the course/project
- ▶ Resourcing

As soon as I had chosen the book, preparing to teach a text to a class seemed overwhelming. Around the time that I began planning for it, our Professional Development committee, of which both Suzy and I were a part, was planning a whole-faculty PD session during which several teachers would present assignments they planned to do with their students to other faculty members. The presenters would share the assignments, answer any clarifying questions, and receive both "warm" (strengths) and "cool" (questions and gaps) feedback, as well as additional suggestions. The committee's purposes for the session were to try to increase the depth of the assignments, anticipate and avoid any foreseeable problems, and attempt to incorporate cross-disciplinary objectives.

It was during this planning session that Suzy urged me to be one of the presenters so that other staff members could share ideas on teaching a book. Although I knew I would be vulnerable to the criticisms and overwhelmed by the many anticipated proposals of colleagues, I craved any help that I could get. So with Suzy's prompting, I agreed.

I shared my project with about 10 other teachers using a modified consultancy protocol (McDonald et al., 2007) during our Professional Development meeting. Many were very enthusiastic to share their ideas. It was both exciting and overwhelming to hear their input. I received concrete ideas that I would adjust and implement, which included doing journals with the students and using Book Based Questions (BBQs; see Chapter 5), for which the students would find evidence within the text to answer broader questions provided by the teacher. I left the consultancy protocol feeling like I had a lot of work ahead of me, but also a solid foundation to begin planning to teach the text. (See Chapter 6 for more about this professional development session.)

Coaching Habit:
- ▶ Making connections, sharing strengths

In early April right before spring break, with much grumbling about the assignment they had just received, my students began reading *Nickel and Dimed*. In our weekly planning meetings, Suzy encouraged me to get my students' e-mail addresses so that I could e-mail them over break reminding them to read the assigned portion. As they read the book, they were to mark with a "sticky" (Post-it) any part they wanted to discuss later in class, any question they had, or any word of which they were unsure of the definition. This would ensure that they were actively reading. Students also had to complete a few BBQs by using examples within the book to answer questions I posed. They would journal periodically as they read, trying to predict whether or not Barbara (the author) would be able to live on wages she received, or problems that she might face, or what they would do differently in her situation. Finally, the students took multiple-choice quizzes every few days to test their reading comprehension.

When the project had been completed, I felt like it had been a success on some levels and a failure on others. Being able to incorporate a relatively lengthy text into the curriculum felt like a huge accomplishment. My students had read very few full texts throughout their high school experiences, so to provide one for them felt exciting as I was helping them better prepare for postsecondary education, and making their academics at Park East more enriching. There had been some really great discussions spurred by the varied experiences Barbara described in the book. I vividly remember one discussion we had that was stimulated by the students. We had just begun a read-aloud of Chapter 3, which began:

> I had thought for months of going to Sacramento or somewhere else in California's Central Valley not far from Berkeley, where I'd spent the spring. But warnings about the heat and the allergies put me off, not to mention my worry that the Latinos might be hogging all the crap jobs and substandard housing for themselves as they so often do. (p. 121)

A few gasps were heard, and one student raised his hand, "Ms. Reist, is she a racist?" Rather than responding myself, many of my students quickly jumped in to answer. There were about five students actively engaged in the discussion, each with a different perspective on the question. The students were able to support their positions with real-life experiences and other excerpts from the book.

It was encouraging to see a few of them become animated as they commented or made remarks about how they had enjoyed the book. When we had completed the book, the students were angry about the reality of the author's conclusion that it was next to impossible to live on low wages. "Ms. Reist, why did we read this? . . . We already knew this."

After hearing some of their complaints, I had an idea to write a senator asking for an increase in the minimum wage. This was one way we could at least attempt to remedy the problems that had been described in the book and to use evidence from the text to do so.

The students decided to send their letters to Senator Hillary Rodham Clinton. In the letters, I asked them to summarize the book, address three issues of concern about low-wage labor raised in the book, and call her to action to raise the minimum wage. The students were also able to apply aspects of the book to their lives in the letters they wrote. In asking Senator Clinton to fight to raise the minimum wage, they articulated both arguments from the book and personal experiences.

However, I did have some feelings of failure and disappointment as well. Yes, there were students who really were interested in the book and had read it. And all of my students did some reading—those parts we did in class. But it was made evident who had read the book through class discussions and the various assessments, and I could tell that many more students did not read more than those parts we did in the class. They were quick to complain, and could not understand why they were being "forced" to read what they already knew, that "low-wage labor 'sucks.'"

I would tell them, "Yes, you may be able to say that, but you need to have concrete evidence to make your arguments credible. And you must know causes and effects of low-wage labor, and consider possible solutions to its consequences."

Was it a failure on my part that the students viewed the book so negatively? Was it a lack of planning? Maybe. I did not collect their journals regularly to provide personal feedback, the letter to Senator Clinton was somewhat of an afterthought, and maybe there should have been a greater culminating project. Perhaps I failed to hold them accountable enough for doing the reading. Despite my feelings of shortcoming, Suzy was still thrilled that our students had an opportunity to read a text within a social studies classroom.

Coaching Habit:
▶ Sharing enthusiasm

Teaching to a Text: Take Two

Overall I discovered that I liked teaching to a text. It was a lot of preliminary work, but it was something that had the potential to relate more to the students than other lessons. So I decided to improve upon my mistakes, and by late spring asked Suzy what text would be appropriate to incorporate into my eleventh-grade United States history course in the coming fall semester. I had taught the course my first year, and wanted to supplement the lesson plans I had already used with a novel. I felt that the period of Reconstruction was one in which I could use a narrative. I had read Zora Neale Hurston's *Their Eyes Were Watching God* (1937) in a college English course, and wondered if this would be appropriate. Suzy agreed that this would be appropriate when I asked her for her opinion on the text.

Once again I felt overwhelmed when the time came to plan and prepare how the novel would be taught. I knew that it was necessary to provide more structure and scaffold for students this time. My first step after rereading it was to decide what the learning objectives were for the novel. Two that I thought were important were the expectations of African-American women and racial politics of the South in the late 1800s. Suzy helped me shape these themes into the two questions students would have to answer using evidence throughout the whole novel to support their answers:

1. What were expectations of Janie and other Black women in the late 1800s in the South?
2. In what ways does race influence Janie's life experiences?

In addition to the two overarching themes, there were smaller assignments every few chapters to provide structure, focus, and accountability to students' reading.

I felt like I had a good start on the project, but what Suzy told me next was something I did not want to hear. She said it was "imperative" that I include a culminating paper in which students could answer one of two topics based on the overarching themes. I begrudgingly agreed that it was necessary, but did not look forward to developing the writing assignment or the grading that would follow. With the help of Suzy, and based on the two original questions, I formed the two required questions from which students would choose one to form their thesis. Then they had to choose three of five corresponding questions that I asked to help them argue their thesis. These questions were very closely related to the homework assignments—made up mostly of BBQs—so that it provided in some form accountability to their reading.

Coaching Habits:
▶ Framing questions
▶ Pushing for student products

Even once the assignment had been created, I was unsure how to help the students outline their papers. Suzy talked me through scaffolding the assignment for them. She suggested I spend a class period letting the students choose their topic (Required Question 1 or 2) and formulate their theses. The next step would be to have students choose which three questions of the five provided would support their theses and provide a graphic organizer that would allow them to extract specific evidence to support their answers and ultimately their theses.

Suzy was able to walk me through the process by talking about each step of the scaffolding for the project, alleviating much anxiety. Although I had done much of the project independently, including creating assignments and a final paper, Suzy pushed me further than I would have gone on my own, helped finesse the project, and was able to relieve much stress felt prior to and during the planning process.

Coaching Habit:
▶ Problem-solving

I introduced the project to my three classes in mid-December. The students complained immediately as I handed out the outline, with anticipated due dates, the first assignment, which dealt with the first few chapters of the novel, and the culminating paper assignment (see Fig. 4.2). I read the first chapter aloud to the classes. Then I had them guess what the story might entail, and many were interested from the very beginning.

Teaching this book seemed much more successful than *Nickel and Dimed*. Just like with the first book, my students had the opportunity to read a complete text. It provided practice for writing papers and supporting theses. However, this time more students handed in the assignments. Many were very curious about the plot of the story, and asked questions about the main character, Janie. A few students enjoyed reading aloud to their peers, even with the difficult vernacular. Some days the bell would ring, and students would let out a sigh of disappointment that we had to stop reading at that point. This elated me as a teacher, and I had a great experience sharing this story with my students, while providing a break from the regular curriculum. Finally, it was very welcoming and refreshing to hear students voice excitement and interest about what we were doing.

Not all aspects of teaching *Their Eyes Were Watching God* were positive. I still had the problem of some students not reading or doing the assignments. The rough drafts were mediocre, and many students neglected to use evidence collected to support their theses. So another scaffolding step was added between the rough and final drafts, in which they had to use each argument and state how each supported their theses, something I thought up and ran past Suzy. By the time I received their final essays, there was a greater depth of analysis, and nice use of evidence to validate their arguments.

It was also a lot of work for me. Much of it was work done in advance, by me and in my planning with Suzy. However, the grading and checking of assignments became tedious and mundane early on. Even so, it was worth doing, not just from the standpoint that it provided the opportunity

Figure 4.2. Paper Assignment: *Their Eyes Were Watching God*

Name:
U.S. History
Park East High School

Directions: This paper is based on the book *Their Eyes Were Watching God*. You will choose one of the following tasks and write a well-organized essay that includes an introduction, several body paragraphs addressing the task below, and a conclusion.

Question 1

Context: Throughout the novel we have been discussing the gender expectations that others placed on Janie.

Task: Discuss what Zora Neale Hurston is telling us about the expectations and life of black women in the South after the Civil War by (1) Answering the required question (2) Answering 3 of the 5 following questions.

REQUIRED

"Ships at a distance have every man's wish on board. For some they come in with the tide. For others they sail forever on the horizon, never out of sight, never landing until the Watcher turns his eyes away in resignation, his dreams mocked to death by Time. That is the life of men.

"Now, women forget all those things they don't want to remember, and remember everything they don't want to forget. The dream is the truth. Then they act and do things accordingly." (page 1)

Do you agree with the sentiment in this quotation, that women can control their wills and chase their dreams, based on Janie's life experiences in *Their Eyes Were Watching God*?

CHOOSE 3 OF 5

- What were Janie's dreams?
- What were Nanny's expectations of Janie and why did she hold these expectations?
- What were Jody's expectations of Janie?
- How did Tea Cake treat Janie differently than her first two husbands?
- From the evidence in the book and your knowledge of history, what were the expectations of Janie and other Black women in the late 1800s in the South?

(continued)

Figure 4.2. (*continued*)

Question 2

Context: Throughout the novel we have been discussing how race places a role in Janie's life.

Task: Discuss what Zora Neale Hurston is telling us about race and how it had an effect on Janie and black women in the South after the Civil War by (1) Answering the required question (2) Answering 3 of the 5 following questions.

REQUIRED

> " . . . Maybe it's some place way off in de ocean where de black man is in power, but we don't know nothin' but what we see. So de white man throw down de load and tell de nigger man tuh pick it up. He pick it up because he have to, but he don't tote it. He hand it to his womenfolks. De nigger woman is de mule uh de world so fur as Ah can see. Ah been prayin' fuh it tuh be different wid you. Lawd, Lawd, Lawd!" (page 14)

In what ways does this quotation, which expresses the idea that black women bear the weight of the world, reflect and shape Janie's life experiences in *Their Eyes Were Watching God*?

CHOOSE 3 OF 5

- What was Janie's reaction when she found out she wasn't white, and how did the other children treat her because of her "finer" clothes?
- What were Logan's expectations of Janie by the end of their marriage?
- Why was Mrs. Turner angry with Janie for being married to Tea Cake?
- What were the expectations of black women in the South?
- In what ways does race influence Janie's life experiences?

Guidelines:

In your essay be sure to:
- Address all aspects of the task
- Support the theme with relevant QUOTES, details, and evidence
- Use traditional format: Introduction (with thesis), Body, Conclusion
- You must correctly cite at least 5 quotes from *Their Eyes Were Watching God* in your paper to support your arguments.
- Use information from class discussions and BBQs
- Type your final paper in Times New Roman 12 Font
- Double Space your Final Draft
- Follow the Rubric to make sure you include all necessary information
- Write at least 500 words (approximately 2 pages)

Timetable:

1/10: Assignment Given; Pre-Write 1
1/11: Pre-Write Day 2
1/16: Rough Copy Due
2/5: Final Draft Due

to enhance my essential instructional skills, but because it allowed me to teach and relate to my students in a new way that I found pleasurable. Without Suzy's coaching and prompting, I would have missed out on this experience. Now I feel more comfortable not only teaching texts, but branching out in a variety of new mediums.

A new semester has begun in the past few weeks. I am teaching economics now for the second time. Right before the semester began, I sat down with Suzy to sketch out a rough calendar and outline of the course. One of the major themes is, "Does Our Market Economy Allow for Social Mobility?" I am planning on incorporating *Nickel and Dimed* again. I will make additions to the assignments and create a final paper to avoid some of the problems of last year. We will also explore excerpts from other texts to address this theme. I feel extremely excited to hear my students' responses once they have been given the chance to weigh the different information. Last year at this time, teaching economics was something I loathed. Now there is an anticipation that I have not felt for any other of the three courses I have taught at Park East.

Coaching Habits Examined

Jennie's story illustrates many of the same coaching habits we saw in Alexis's story above, although in some cases with different emphases given the unique needs of a new teacher, as well as a different subject.

Outlining the Project/Course. For Jennie, a new teacher at the school, and what's more, teaching a brand-new course, it was particularly important for Suzy to help her outline the entire economics course. In the course of creating the outline, Suzy was able to suggest the idea of teaching a complete book as part of the course. When teachers plan week to week and lesson to lesson, it is unlikely that they will be able to realize possibilities for longer-term student projects like reading a book. Creating an outline that breaks the project down into manageable steps can also alleviates the teacher's feelings of being overwhelmed. As Jennie developed her own capacity to plan instruction, she still found it helpful in alleviating her anxiety to talk through each step of the project with Suzy.

Framing Questions. When Jennie decided, with Suzy's enthusiastic support, to introduce a full book, *Their Eyes Were Watching God*, into her U.S. history course, Suzy worked with her to help take her reasons for teaching the book, including ideas about expectations for African-American women in the 1800s, and transform them into questions that would express the overarching themes for the unit and serve as a framework for large and small assignments for the unit.

Pushing for Student Products. Along with introducing questions to guide the reading and student response to the book, Suzy told Jennie it was "imperative" to include an analytical paper within the unit on *Their Eyes*. For Suzy, it is not the requirement for a paper per se that matters, but the development of a product that is a "summation event," that helps students and the teacher "reflect on and tie together" what is learned in reading and discussing the book.

Resourcing. Once Jennie agreed to consider including a book in her curriculum, Suzy shared a number of possible titles, from which Jennie chose *Nickel and Dimed*. It is probably no coincidence that this was the book Suzy recommended, and that Jennie would rely on Suzy's recommendation for the first book. When Jennie decides to introduce a book into her U.S. history class, she chooses the book herself, and Suzy supports her in her choice.

Problem-Solving. Problem-solving does not always occur in response to an "Oh, s---, what do we do now?" problem. It is a regular part of planning and carrying out any meaningful longer-term project. In Jennie's story, one place where this kind of anticipated but no less important problem-solve appears is when Suzy works with Jennie to figure out the optimal way for her U.S. history students to combine their identified thesis question with a certain number of BBQ questions that will serve as scaffolding.

Sharing Enthusiasm. Once again, Suzy works with someone initially resistant to coaching and supports her to move outside her instructional comfort zone. It is an incremental process: once initial steps are taken on the first book and Jennie sees some positive outcomes, she is ready to take additional steps, such as adding the analytical paper when she teaches the second book. Throughout the process, Suzy's enthusiasm provides Jennie with a bulwark of support, even when some of the results are disappointing, as when Jennie realizes during the economics book reading that many students are not keeping up with the reading.

Making Connections, Sharing Strengths. An important part of coaching is keeping your eyes open and seizing on possible opportunities to connect one teacher's work with something else going in another teacher's class or within the school (and sometimes outside it). While planning the unit on *Nickel and Dimed*, Suzy and Jennie were both at the PD committee meeting when the idea was considered for a whole-staff PD in which teachers would share curriculum plans and get feedback from colleagues using a protocol. Suzy encouraged Jennie to present her plan for the book reading in one of the protocols, and as Jennie describes, doing so contributed to the development of the project. (We'll take a closer look at coaching as facilitating connections and collaboration in the next two chapters.)

TEACHING WRITING TRANSFORMED (JOE)

Joe was a third-year social studies teacher when he began working with Suzy as his instructional coach. He had worked with her previously, but as part of the ninth-grade team rather than individually. In this story, Joe describes how, over time, his approach to teaching writing was transformed through his collaboration with Suzy and, eventually, other teachers at the school. As we have seen in the earlier stories, Joe entered into the coaching relationship with some trepidation.

When I started teaching at Park East I was in a conundrum. As a social studies teacher, I wanted the students to pass the Regents exam in U.S. history required for graduation. I also wanted to present content that the students were inherently connected with. It was difficult to juggle those two divergent strands. In addition, as a neophyte teacher, I clung to the belief that no matter what school I taught in, I would make writing a priority in my classroom. After being assigned to Park East I quickly realized that writing was not a priority in the school. Early on I struggled to find a balance between presenting material to properly prepare students for the Regents exam and lessons the students would feel connected with their real world situations. However, my plans to have the students do substantive writing sputtered. I wanted the students to write, but my assignments failed miserably.

Unfortunately, one of my natural strengths is not organization, nor is it planning. I was someone who existed in an extemporaneous world of free association and "teachable moments." During my second year at Park East, I wrote out my first lengthy writing assignment for my ninth-grade U.S. History I class on the subway on the way to work one morning. In total, I spent less than 5 minutes planning the assignment. Due to my inexperience and lack of planning or foresight, my writing assignment looked something like:

In a well-researched essay please answer the question:

Did the "peculiar institution" cause the Civil War? What role did chattel slavery play in shaping Northern and Southern attitudes towards each other leading up to the Civil War?

Final Draft due December 16

My expectation was that students would be able to address this topic on their own time out of school with very little direct assistance or scaffolding from the instructor. In fact, I expected the students at Park East to write independently in much the same way as my high school instructors expected me to complete assignments on my own. One or two linked questions, I believed, would suffice to prompt Park East students to craft a 500-word essay. I was wrong.

I gave the students 2 weeks to write a final draft of the essay. I made an allowance of 1 week in the computer room, to complete research on the Internet, the rest was to be written on their own time. I handed the essay out on December 2, and I expected the class to hand me finished typewritten drafts on the second Monday, December 16.

On Tuesday, December 3, we headed into the computer room. The first research day was a disaster, and a more experienced or intuitive practitioner would have recognized the need to adjust the lessons for the week. I did not. By the end of Tuesday's session half the class was off topic looking up Jay-Z, Aaliyah, and Fat Joe lyrics on the computers. One quarter of the class had a hard time finding their way on to the Internet. The final quarter tried valiantly to find information on Web sites although they had a difficult time deciding if those sites had valid or credible evidence. By Friday, 3 students out of 25 had opted to stay the course and were working on the project; most had completely given up and were utterly dejected—so was their teacher.

The following week I spent one class period going over the writing of the paper. I explained my criteria for grading. We discussed what a proper thesis should look like. My lack of clarity on grading expectations and convoluted discussion of a "thesis" guaranteed that all but the most astute were now completely lost by this assignment. I can still remember asking the students, "Do you understand that a thesis clarifies for the reader what your argument is?" The vacant stares and absence of questions from the students should have been a clarion blast that something was totally amiss. If not these expressions, then Alex sleeping on the desk next to the board should have been a clue. On the paper's due date I received five typed "final" drafts and one handwritten essay.

The project failed. I was unwilling to accept responsibility for the failure and, instead, talked myself into the conclusion that the need to focus on the Regents exam meant there was not enough time to take on any long-term writing assignments; to do so would mean foregoing content in my history courses. My writing priority was quickly jettisoned after one meager attempt. The students would write in their English courses. If the students were going to write in my class it was only going to be on exams without any revision and it would only be directly connected to Regents-type questions, "Document Based Questions" (DBQ), and "Thematic Essays." For the remainder of the year through U.S. History II, the only writing the students did was on exams.

Creating a Dialogue About Teaching

The following year I taught the same group of students, now in the 11th grade, for Global History, meeting with the students for a double period (90 minutes) every day. Suzy's coaching role had expanded beyond the ninth-grade team, and so I was scheduled to work with Suzy.

It was a natural fit for Suzy to work with me as my instructional coach: I was a novice social studies teacher and Suzy had been a social studies teacher before becoming a coach. Even so, at first I was very hesitant to work with Suzy in this capacity. I did not wish to open my classroom to anyone (especially an outsider, as I viewed Suzy at this juncture). Often I found reasons to miss or skip our scheduled meetings. Suzy was a tenacious coach, however. She would not accept my attempts to dodge our meetings; eventually she was able to track me down, and I began to meet with her more regularly. I often wonder what would have happened if Suzy had been more passive.

By the middle of the year, we had a routine of meeting weekly for a period of planning. We would gradually begin to communicate in other ways as well; for example, at this point, it was not unusual for me to call her on a Saturday or Sunday to run by her an idea for a lesson I might have.

During our first year of working together, once we were meeting regularly, Suzy suggested that she could help me to design a writing project for my Global History courses. I balked. "I don't have the time." "There is way too much content for me to cover." "The students already write for me on exams." These were all excuses that I used to cover the fact that I was afraid to attempt another writing project with the same students I had failed to properly instruct during a writing project the year before. Exhibiting more tenacity, Suzy refused to accept my excuses—she chipped away at my reluctance.

Coaching Habits:
▶ Persisting
▶ Pushing for student products
▶ Communicating regularly

Suzy was able to identify tactics to have conversations about writing without directly forcing me to confront my fears. She would have conversations with me about the importance of literacy and writing as a larger social problem. To this day I think those conversations were planned and intentional. Suzy recognized that I still believed that writing and literacy instruction were the most important facets of a quality high school education, even if in my own practice I often failed to implement much of either. Our conversations about writing became regular parts of our meetings, and after about a month of prodding, I relented.

Suzy would never have said at first something to the effect of, "You need to have the students do a writing project this marking period." If she had said something like that to me early on, I would have walked away from any type of collaboration with her. Instead she took a gradual approach—what in deference to her idol, Bill Clinton, she refers to as an "incremental approach." Over the next few months our planning sessions focused on developing workable assignments.

Coaching Habits:
▶ Building incrementally
▶ Framing questions

Realizing that I would be most comfortable assigning projects that were within the Global Studies curriculum, Suzy suggested that I assign the students document-based question (DBQ) essays, a staple of the Regents curriculum. The first essay I assigned was about world religions. I worked on creating a central idea and context for the assignment. I also identified some documents that could be easily analyzed and synthesized by the students. Suzy worked with me to craft subquestions for each document. I was used to teaching documents in class and creating DBQ essays for exams, so the first essay assignment was not much of a stretch. Once the assignment was created, Suzy stated that a timetable for the project and a heading to the assignment would be welcome additions. I made the additions. The paper minus the documents appears in Figure 4.3 (with apologies to the New York State Board of Regents).

Suzy suggested that when I initially handed students the assignment I spend one class period going over the assignment with the students. Looking back to my failed attempts the previous year, I readily agreed.

Figure 4.3. Essay III—Document Based Essay

Park East High School
Global History I–II
11/10/03

Essay III—Document Based Essay

Directions: Write a well organized essay that includes an introduction, several body paragraphs addressing the task below and a conclusion.

Historical Context:

Throughout history, religion/belief systems has (have) influenced mankind and the world's diverse cultures. Since the first River Valley Civilizations, religious beliefs have united and divided people. The world's great religions, Islam, Judaism, Buddhism, Hinduism and Christianity, have helped to create peace and order; however, they have also created warfare and destruction. Organized religion has helped to define almost every era in World History.

Task:

Chose three religions and for each:

- Describe why specific Religions developed and who helped to develop them
- Discuss how Religion created order and excluded nonbelievers
- Analyze what purpose you believe religion serves in world history

Guidelines:

In your essay be sure to:

- Address all aspects of the task
- Support your argument about the topic with relevant facts, examples, details and evidence
- Use traditional format: Intro (with a Thesis), Body, Conclusion
- You must cite at least 5 documents in your paper
- Use at least 5 quotes from the documents
- Type your paper in Times New Roman 12 Font
- Follow the Rubric to make sure you include all necessary information
- Write AT LEAST 500 WORDS

Timetable:

11/10: Paper assigned
11/19: Rough Drafts to be handed in to Mr. Schmidt
11/24: Corrected Rough Drafts to be returned
 12/1: Final Copies due

The results were evident in the clarity of students' questions about the assignment; I could see from their questions that students realized the assignment could be used to frame out the parts of the essay, and that they were going to be able to complete this essay more easily on their own.

Small suggestions such as this made the difference between a successful writing assignment and a failed one. When the due date arrived, the 25% of the class turning in a final draft from the previous year turned into 75%. While far from perfect—many still lacked a thesis—most essays included evidence from the documents and clearer organization.

I identify two changes that I made for this assignment that helped to make it successful. The first change was that both the assignment and the way I presented it to students were scaffolded to help foster students' understanding of the project. The documents I gave the students were developed in order to help the students to write the essay and incorporate evidence from said documents. When I discussed the assignment with the students, our discussion mirrored the scaffolded way in which Suzy helped me to build the project. The first step led to a second step, which led to a third, and so on.

The second major change was that within the timetable for the paper I included a period for revision. I spent roughly one week making corrections on a first draft. The students were then expected to use the corrections and suggestions to craft their final drafts. Suzy was adamant that these paper assignments should include a period of revision. She was right: To this day I include a revision step in every paper assignment I give.

Raising the Stakes

After the success of this paper assignment, I think Suzy waited a week before stating, "You should give one paper assignment every marking period." Forget the incremental approach! Once Suzy had won me over through gentle cajoling and meeting with me in my comfort zone, she then pushed me, although never too far, to increase my expectations of the students and my expectations of their teacher. Once she had a clear success to point to, and it became clear to me that working with a coach had value, our meetings and working relationship developed more fully.

Thinking about this chapter, I was perusing some of my e-mails to Suzy (who regularly e-mails teachers she works with as well as holding myriad phone conversations). I happened to find an early e-mail to Suzy dated February 11 with the subject "I e-mail . . . sometimes." Though brief, it is very telling for a variety of reasons:

Suzy,
'Cause we never met today, and 'cause I'm kind of proud of the DBQ
I wrote . . . here it is.

js

p.s. not a word to anyone at P.E. that I use e-mail.

This e-mail is illustrative of Suzy's impact as a coach. First, it clearly shows that, following the first two assignments I crafted with her, by the third paper I was working on the assignment on my own and asking Suzy to look it over before I gave it to the students. My e-mail also shows how Suzy always maintains an ongoing conversation with the teachers she works with even on days when she is unable to meet with them. Finally, the tone in my e-mail indicates that Suzy was able to gain my trust and willing involvement in our collaboration. This is quite a change from the previous October, when I actively sought to avoid our scheduled meetings. Suzy used our discussions about writing projects to develop a successful relationship that continues to this day.

Coaching Habits:
▶ Communicating regularly
▶ Sharing enthusiasm

Expanding Practices

I still work regularly with Suzy, collaborating on lessons and writing projects. During my fourth year, under Suzy's guidance, I was able to assign a paper every marking period for the entire year and still prepare the students for the Regents exam. In fact, Suzy helped me to recognize that in moving away from teaching to the test I would better benefit the students by better preparing them for their lives after high school.

Suzy also suggested that I expand my practice and take on the challenge of the interdisciplinary humanities course we began offering. By co-teaching humanities, I learned along with my co-teacher, Drew Allsopp, to frame paper assignments that asked the students to develop arguments in response to larger thematic questions, as well as to develop a clear system to gather evidence from texts that would be employed to bolster their arguments—smaller assignments we called BBQs, or Book-based Questions (see Chapter 5).

Suzy would regularly meet with Drew and me to think through the paper assignments. These assignments, while still tangentially connected to the Regents Global Studies curriculum, were much more clearly articulated than the DBQ-type essays I had crafted in years past. Suzy also brought in another coach who was a literacy and writing specialist to help us further plan our assignments. Quite a bit had changed for me since I wrote the Civil War essay assignment one morning on the subway coming into work. Drew and I would often discuss the essay assignment for a couple of weeks together and then hone it with Suzy and Phyllis, the ISA literacy coach.

Coaching Habits:
▶ Making connections, sharing strengths
▶ Resourcing

Over the course of the 5 years that I have worked with Suzy, my ability to create well-planned, thoughtful writing assignments has increased tremendously. I no longer hide behind excuses as to why I cannot give writing assignments in a history course. In fact, in the fall of 2006, I threw out a large portion of the Global Studies III curriculum so that the students could read *The Tempest* and write essays on Shakespeare's portrayal of colonialism and the treatment of the "other" as embodied by Caliban. I attribute that change in pedagogical approach to my work with Suzy.

Coaching Habits Examined

Once again, in Joe's story, we see the same importance of outlining, problem-solving, pushing for student products, framing questions, and resourcing described in the sections following Alexis' and Jennie's stories. As Joe's story develops over time, it is especially helpful in calling out coaching habits that themselves develop over the course of a longer period. For this reason, we highlight three of the habits that are most important to building a relationship that supports a teacher's growth.

Persisting. Joe's account demonstrates the coach's indefatigable perseverance. When Suzy was first assigned to work with Joe, he did his best to avoid working with her: "Most people would have given up on a recalcitrant one such as me. Suzy was willing to work at developing an entrée to a working relationship." Coaches encounter many teachers who at first seem or are resistant to working with them. In Joe's case, Suzy demonstrated a willingness to come back again and again. Equally important was the coach's ability to identify an *entry point* for discussing instructional change, Joe's interest in literacy and writing "as a larger social problem," without which there would have been no genuine context for Suzy's "prodding" and "chipping away"—a term Alexis also used.

Building Incrementally. In her work with Jennie, we saw Suzy's insistence on incorporating a research paper in only her second whole-book reading project. Joe points out that with him, "Suzy started slowly. The first papers were content and curriculum specific, and later she made suggestions that I increase the frequency and difficulty of the assignments." Suzy describes this aspect of her coaching as knowing what a teacher, or a school, for that matter, is ready to "pull off," and building from there.

Communicating Regularly. In all three stories, we have seen examples of Suzy's commitment to ongoing communication with the teachers she plans with. The scheduled face-to-face meetings are, of course, critical to the planning process. Equally important is the encouragement for teachers to e-mail and call her—with the certainty that they'll get an *enthusiastic* and helpful response. In Chapter 3, Suzy discusses how she organizes her time to make these kinds of communication possible.

The stories told by Alexis, Jennie, and Joe offer rich examples of how educators collaborate with the coach to develop stronger instructional units for their students and to develop their own instructional planning skills. In each case, it is often impossible to identify where the coach's or the teacher's ideas leave off and the other's begins in planning. Suzy looks for the same kind of collaborative opportunities *among* teachers, as she did in encouraging Jennie to present her plan in the PD session protocol. She has encouraged Joe to collaborate with other teachers, as he did with Drew in taking on the humanities course, and work with other coaches such as Phyllis Tashlik, the ISA literacy coach. In Chapter 6, we take a closer look at the coaching emphasis on deepening collaboration among teachers.

CHAPTER 5

Complementary Strategies

Planning, the focus of our previous chapter, is at the heart of the coach's support for teachers' development of curriculum and instruction; it both provides material for teachers to use immediately in their classes and models and develops the skills and habits necessary to plan on their own and with colleagues. However, planning does not stand on its own as a coaching strategy but gains power when combined with a number of other practices we describe in this chapter. These include observing teachers in classrooms; feeding teachers with resources; checking in with teachers about instructional questions and organizational issues; and making connections and sharing strengths. In this chapter, we examine these coaching strategies and identify some of the key coaching habits associated with each, many of which have been discussed in detail in the previous chapters—new habits are discussed following each section.

OBSERVING CLASSROOMS

Observing teachers in their classrooms and providing feedback in a postobservation discussion is a common coaching strategy, especially in content coaching models, such as literacy or math coaching. As we described in Chapter 2, early on in Suzy's coaching, she spent more of her time at the school in teachers' classrooms and meeting with them afterward to debrief. In some cases, she was there as an observer; in others, she was more actively involved, as she put it, "just being another adult body [in the room] helping the students stay on task, and in some cases assisting with classroom management." In each case, she was in a position to observe the teacher's instructional strengths and needs, which provided useful information for her meetings with the teacher to discuss what was happening in the classroom and plan for future classes.

By Suzy's own account, that planning felt much more useful to her than simply observing and giving feedback based on what she had observed.

Over time her emphasis shifted to planning: Observation went from being Suzy's most frequent coaching strategy in the first year to third most frequent, after planning meetings with individual teachers and committee meetings (see Chapter 3). However, it continued to play an important role in the planning Suzy did with teachers; as she describes:

> I think it is crucial for me to have a feel for how the teacher is in the room, and who particular students are in a class, and a sense of the issues in order to plan effectively for class with teachers. . . . Successful teaching exists within the relationship between the teacher, the material, and the students. I cannot be helpful to a teacher without knowing something about the class.

Some of the typical things Suzy looks for and records during classroom observations include:

- a clear idea guiding the lesson
- a definite task for students to engage in
- participation among a range of students
- circulation, i.e., moving around the room by the teacher
- evidence of organization and classroom routines

One of the questions Suzy asks when she is learning about a teacher's class, through either observation or discussion with the teacher, is what they can "really pull off," in other words, whether the teacher, at this point in their development, has the pedagogical skills, relationships with students, and knowledge of content necessary to undertake more challenging activities and projects.

Coaching Habit:
▶ Setting achievable targets

Suzy reports, "In my experience, a big disconnect between talk and action has been rare. For the most part, when there is a trusting relationship [between teacher and coach] and the planning is useful to the teacher, there is no incentive for misrepresentation; rather, we work together work to solve the puzzle of teaching."

Even so, it is often helpful to see teachers in their classrooms rather than rely on their descriptions of "what they do and how it goes." For example, in a brief observation of the last few minutes of Alexis's anatomy class, during one of her periodic sweeps, Suzy was able to see (not for the first time) how effective Alexis was in evoking and responding to students' questions, for example, about the human body's muscle groups, the topic of that day's class. As she sat in the back of the room, she noted this aspect of Alexis's teaching in her ever-present notebook and, on her way out the door, complimented her on it.

Coaching Habit:
▶ Sharing enthusiasm

Later in the day, during a regular planning meeting with Alexis, most of which was devoted to planning a Student Life committee activity, Suzy brought up an idea for her anatomy class that she had discussed earlier of using a recurring question, "What goes wrong?," as a lens for student inquiry. Alexis responded that she had incorporated the question as part of students' regular homework assignments. Their discussion reflected Suzy's sense that Alex is ready—can pull off—bigger questions and more independent research for students, although at this point Alexis was still cautious about incorporating a project of the size Suzy envisioned and preferred to limit the use of the lens to homework assignments. (See Chapter 4 for Alexis's story about incorporating a student project in her teaching.)

Other Ways of Seeing a Classroom

To see a teacher in his or her classroom does not always mean sitting in the back of the room for a full period taking notes—or even for a few minutes, as in the example from Alexis's anatomy class above. Suzy describes some of the many ways a coach can be in the classroom:

> I tend to drop into classes for short periods of time or participate in classes as requested by a teacher—sometimes to help launch a project we have planned together, such as a solar system modeling project I have worked on with a new earth science teacher. I have also joined classes on occasion to read aloud to students or as a "guest speaker" on topics I know well to provide [students with] a college-style lecture opportunity.

Suzy recounted a more extensive and systematic example of classroom observation when Joe, a social studies teacher turned for the semester into an English teacher, asked her to observe his class weekly, in place of their usual meeting time, to note opportunities for democratic discussion. Joe describes his motivation for inviting Suzy to observe and offer feedback with a specific objective in mind:

> I recognize that I am naturally inclined to fostering a teacher-centered traditional classroom. When I began teaching a senior

elective literature class, I decided I wanted to make a concerted effort to open up the class discussion and to take the focus away from me and shift it to class discussion around thought-provoking and academically challenging questions.

I also wanted someone to keep track of how many students were involved in the discussions. I asked Suzy if she could observe my class once a week and keep track of two questions, one purely by tally, the other with some qualitative observations: Was a large portion of the class taking part in the discussion regularly? Were students at the center of the class discussion? She and I would then try to meet once a week so she could give me feedback.

Coaching Habit:
▶ Debriefing

Coaching Habits Examined

Two new coaching habits are introduced above: *setting achievable targets* and *debriefing* instruction. A common refrain in Suzy's coaching is the question, "What can we pull off?" The point of the question is set, concrete, achievable targets for instruction—ones with a high degree of "do-ability." Rather than setting limits on a teacher's instructional practice, the question helps to identify a zone within which the teacher working with Suzy can expand his or her instructional repertoire.

Debriefing instruction is an important complement to observing teachers teach. Like setting achievable targets, a key to effective debriefing is to figure out where teachers are in their instructional development and provide the feedback that they are ready for and will benefit from receiving. Suzy often begins a debriefing discussion by asking the teacher whose class she has observed, "How did it go?" and works from there.

PROVIDING RESOURCES

Suzy is fond of saying that one of the most important things she does as a coach is read the *New York Times* every day. Of course, it is not the habitual reading that contributes to her coaching but how she uses the newspaper and other media as potential resources for the teachers she works with. She regularly clips articles and puts them in teachers' boxes with a brief note, for example, "FYI, thought you might be interested for gov't class on an article about states considering lowering the voting age to 16." Or she will bring the paper open to a particular article or advertisement to a planning meeting with a teacher.

An episode of resourcing occurred one morning when Suzy met with Joe and Drew during first period to plan their humanities class project on *Animal Farm*. While waiting for Drew and making small talk over coffee, Suzy told Joe about an article from that morning's paper about the many letters to Shakespeare's Juliet left by visitors at the Metropolitan Museum model of Juliet's house in the play. She mentioned that it might be useful for a future class activity when teaching the play. Joe looked at the paper and told her he was actually more interested in a television documentary about Eugene O'Neill reviewed on the same page. When Drew arrived, Suzy reported Joe's lack of interest in the story and passed the paper to Drew, who glanced at the page and remarked, "Hey, there's a new Ghostface Killah CD."

While nothing except some good-natured teasing came out of this pitch by Suzy, the practice of feeding teachers with resources from the paper and other sources often pays off. In another case, Suzy brought a story about *Bodies*, an exhibition of preserved human bodies then opening for the first time in New York City. According to Suzy, "Alexis grumbled, but she read." Later, when students brought Alexis an ad from the free subway newspaper and asked if they could go, "Alexis was pleased she knew about it beforehand. Now it is a tradition in the Anatomy class; we have gone at least five times. Now they can't wait to go."

Alexis has come to appreciate the value of using outside resources to scaffold her instruction:

> Following Suzy's lead with the *New York Times*, I am now a subscriber to *National Geographic*, in which I have found articles that relate to my own curriculum as well as to the curricula of my colleagues in both the science and social studies departments. Plus I have actually read articles thinking this would be great for Joe's Global class and brought him in the article, for example, one about the Mayans.

The *Times* is far from being the only source of resources Suzy monitors for the teachers she works with. Catalogs of instructional materials provide another rich vein of possible ideas and physical resources. In Chapter 4, Alexis describes how perusing a catalog of science teaching materials with Suzy played a key role in the water study she conducted with her students.

Some other examples of resources Suzy has fed teachers with include:

- Seeing the production of *A Raisin in the Sun* (Hansberry) with Sean Combs to tie in with reading the play
- A unit on the Electoral College based on a *New York Times* editorial

- A study of population decline supported by an article on Easter Island from the *New York Times*
- Reading books such as *Maggie, Girl of the Streets* (Stephen Crane), *Nickel and Dimed* (Barbara Ehrenreich), *Jazz* (Toni Morrison), *Persepolis* (Marjane Satrapi), *Candide* (Voltaire), and *Maus* (Art Spiegelman)
- Studying Supreme Court cases such as *Tinker* and *Kyllo vs. United States* (thermal imaging used to detect marijuana)
- Incorporating films such as *Primary Colors* and *Minority Report* for government classes
- Trip ideas: Chelsea Piers (recreation complex) for health, New York Historical Society for U.S. history, Central Park for earth science, etc.

CHECKING IN

As a coach, Suzy works with teachers at widely different levels of experience and with widely different needs. Some teachers, especially newer ones, need more intensive co-planning of curriculum and instruction that we portrayed in Chapter 4. Other teachers are more comfortable with and skilled in planning but still benefit from regular, if less intensive, contact with the coach.

There are a number of teachers at the school whom Suzy regularly checks in with. She might spend as little as 5 or 10 minutes with them during a free period, getting a sense of where they are in their planning and teaching—and what needs they might have. In order to be able to provide these teachers with the resources and feedback they need, based on such a brief interaction, Suzy needs to know their teaching well—knowledge that Suzy developed from spending time in their classrooms (as discussed above), prior planning sessions, and informal conversations.

An Episode of "Microplanning"

An example of checking in as a coaching strategy is Suzy's work with Clancy McKenna, an English teacher who has been at Park East since 2003. In her first year of coaching, Suzy worked with Clancy in weekly planning meetings. In the example below from 3 years later, we present a typical meeting of Suzy and Clancy that happened during Clancy's free period in her classroom. It lasted about 10 minutes, and provides a microcosm of how many coaching habits come together in a very short period.

Clancy is working at her desk when Suzy and David Allen (observing) enter the room. Suzy tells Clancy she left some nutritional newsletters for her in her box (with articles about effects of fats in children's diets for a unit on nutrition and the politics of fast food culture). Clancy explains to David that "Suzy's been helping me work on a project for [high-functioning] seniors," a research paper on controversial issues, including police brutality, raised again after the recent controversial shooting death by detectives of an unarmed man (Sean Bell) at a nightclub in Queens. The senior class is a challenge for Clancy, who has primarily taught ninth graders at the school. She hands Suzy a copy of the handout about the project she has prepared for the students.

Suzy takes a quick look at the sheet. "I would say, from this point, what would somebody who disagrees with you say?"

Clancy responds, "What's the other point of view?"

"That could be your analytic: 'What would the PBA (Policemen's Benevolent Association) say?'"

"Great." Clancy makes notes on her copy of the handout.

Suzy continues, "What would be your—"

Clancy finishes her thought, "your response? Very good! Have them provide evidence."

Suzy and Clancy discuss a timeline for drafts and revisions. Clancy mentions that she would love to be able to conference with her students, and Suzy suggests writing on each student's draft and then conferencing with them.

Clancy, taking more notes, says: "So collect and comment, then conference."

Coaching Habits:
▶ Outlining project/course
▶ Framing questions

Suzy says, "Set a firm deadline, first draft, second draft, final draft." She makes some notes on her copy of the handout. Pointing to one of the classes on the emerging schedule, she says, "Here I'd have a peer review. Jackie Mittman did something like this in PD [staffwide professional development session] last week." She describes how another English teacher had organized her class so that each student's paper cycled through a "checklist thing" for peer-editing. Clancy supplies the word "stations."

Right," Suzy says, "each paper cycled through stations." Their enthusiasm builds as they consider how to build the station idea into Clancy's persuasive writing project. Suzy suggests that Clancy include in the assignment a requirement that the paper "improves each time" (with each draft). Clancy agrees, saying, "I learned with ninth graders that you need to tell them their drafts need to be different."

Suzy suggests putting the final products together in binders as something the students will be proud of, "something they can show visitors." Clancy suggests she can use the finished papers as models for her ninth-grade class in teaching how to write a persuasive piece. Clancy tells David, "I'm big on binders."

Coaching Habits:
▶ Making connections, sharing strengths
▶ Pushing for student products

Suzy tells Clancy she needs "to fly" but on the way out the door has one more idea, perhaps sparked by Clancy's idea of using the papers to model persuasive writing: "Another station could be reading [the paper] with the ISA rubric," which was developed for persuasive writing.

Clancy agrees, "Nice."

Suzy: "Stack the deck a little, put the strongest students with hardest station task."

This very brief and fast-paced interaction suggests how some of the coaching habits and practices we have seen in other contexts can be practiced in very condensed form once a teacher and the coach have developed a trusting relationship and common language about instruction—and when the teacher already has a strong base of planning and instructional skills and knowledge. Though Clancy already had a developed project assignment for her class, she welcomed Suzy's questions and input. For Suzy, "the goal is always to engage the teacher in the intellectual work of preparing for teaching, to share in that thinking process."

Since she was already familiar with Clancy's teaching and had worked with her on similar projects, "I know her and her work and what she's after." Suzy was able to very quickly identify in Clancy's assignment some places where she could go further, especially in terms of using the drafting and revising process to improve the students' writing. Some of the specific ways she did so was through encouraging Clancy to be more explicit and concrete about the timeline and about her expectations for how students' work should develop, for instance, that each draft show progress from the last. Here, Suzy identified her coaching goal as adding analysis to the task.

We can also see the familiar habit in Suzy's coaching of student work products when she encourages Clancy to collect the finished research papers in binders that can be displayed to visitors—and Clancy immediately sees another use for the papers, as models for younger students.

Clancy's project also provided Suzy with an opportunity to model the coaching habit of making connections, here through her practice of facilitating the sharing of teachers' practices. She reminded Clancy of how another English teacher has set up her class to do peer editing through stations. Knowing Clancy's teaching, Suzy was confident that she could pull off everything they discussed.

As Suzy and Clancy work together, it becomes clear that they are "clicking," feeding off each other's ideas, often finishing each other's sentences. The rapid-fire microplanning session seems to build enthusiasm for the project in both.

Other Forms of Checking In

Checking in is a constant aspect of Suzy's work: It happens on both the instructional and organizational levels, and in multiple forms—hallway conversations, e-mail messages, telephone calls. It is often a piece of other kinds of meetings, with Suzy prefacing an idea or questions, "Oh, by the way . . . "

As Suzy gets to know a teacher's strengths and needs, and develops a relationship with that teacher, these brief communiqués can provide teachers with a small but important piece at just the point at which they can use in their instructional planning or delivery. Teachers often initiate these checking-in conversations, for example, the e-mails from Jackie and Brianne we shared in Chapter 3.

Checking in is not limited to instructional concerns—very often it concerns organizational issues—or to teachers, as we will see when we discuss coaching and leadership in Chapter 7. Some other examples of checking in from Suzy's coaching include:

- with an earth science teacher about his activity for field trip to Central Park
- with committee leaders before meetings about the agenda
- before events, if anything needs to be done, for example, calling Alexis to see if we need more Sharpies [markers] for students to write their names on the "WELCOME TO HIGH SCHOOL, CLASS OF 2011," banner.

MAKING CONNECTIONS, SHARING STRENGTHS

In the opening vignettes in Chapter 1, we glimpsed an example of how Suzy looks for possibilities for connecting teachers to one another as resources when Suzy introduced Ed Poli to Brianne Tafuro just before the staff professional development session began. Suzy knew Brianne had completed a project on world religions in which students had produced posters one year and pamphlets another year on religious conflicts throughout the world. She also knew that Ed, with his background in technology, might be able to help Brianne expand on the success of the project by incorporating student-created PowerPoint presentations. It worked. The next time she taught the unit, each student chose a historical theme—technology, geography, political struggle—and created a PowerPoint presentation looking at their theme over time. Ed met with Brianne several times to plan the project and came to class to show the students how to use PowerPoint.

We saw yet another example of making connections in the description of checking in with Clancy when she suggested she "see Jackie Mittman" about how she set up stations for students' revision of their writing.

"Traveling BBQ"

Another example of sharing strengths is found in the story of how the book-based question technique Joe described in Chapter 4 gradually spread to become a model for instruction across the staff. The BBQ is a technique of asking students a broad question about a text and directing them to seek specific examples of evidence in the text in response to the question. Students write down direct quotes from the text that are evidence and locate the quote in the text by page number, as well as where it is located on the page—T, M, B, for top, middle, or bottom. Then they compose an approximately one-page response to the broad question, often in an essay, using the evidence they've amassed.

The BBQ technique proved effective in Joe and Drew's humanities class and Clancy's English classes, and started to show up in other teachers' instruction through a combination of informal sharing, often by Suzy during planning meetings, and more formal PD sessions, including one in which Joe and Drew's *Animal Farm* essay, incorporating three BBQs, was presented in a Tuning Protocol for feedback and discussion (see Chapter 6).

As an outcome of the protocol presentation and coaching discussions, the BBQ has become a model for assessment practice schoolwide. It has helped teachers figure out how to support students in using evidence to make a point or answer a question. According to Suzy, "It put the onus on teachers to create assignments which nudge students to demonstrate their learning rather than just regurgitate. BBQs solidified 'evidence' as part of our lexicon. . . . Some teachers that use the BBQ technique use it over and over again so that it becomes part of the repertoire and students become masters of it." The BBQ has also been adapted for viewing films. See Figure 5.1 for an example BBQ from Joe and Drew's humanities class unit on *Animal Farm.*

Figure 5.1. Sample Book–Based Question (BBQ)

Humanities

Name: _____

Class: A.M._____ P.M._____

Animal Farm BBQ 2: The New Republic

Context: Old Major has described his vision of an ideal farm. Now, the animals begin the process of turning "Manor Farm" into "Animal Farm."

Question: What different actions do the animals perform to support Old Major's ideology of a farm worked and owned by and for animals? Try to find four different actions.

Procedure for BBQs:

1. Read the context and the question.
2. Use the box below to take notes while reading.
3. Answer the question in paragraph form on the back of this page. Direct quotes from the novel, along with explanations, are the best types of evidence to use as evidence. (Ex: On page 18, Old Major says, "_____"
   This shows his support for the new farm by _____)

Page #	T, M, B	Quote/Comments

Response: What different actions do the animals perform to support Old Major's ideology for the new Animal Farm?

Facilitating such teacher-to-teacher connections is effective on multiple levels. It both provides teachers with curriculum resources that have been pilot tested in another teacher's classroom, often on a "just-in-time" basis, and acknowledges the value of teachers' curriculum development at schoolwide level.

Coaching habit:
▶ Recycling

Connecting Outsiders In

Of course, there are beneficial connections beyond those made among peers. An important part of Suzy's work is looking for ways to bring people into the school who can provide resources she may not be able to provide. In this way, the partnership with ISA has been especially profitable, since ISA maintains content-area coaches who are available to work with partner schools to support teachers as needed for their development of inquiry curriculum and instruction. Suzy has reached out to ISA to collaborate with these coaches in a number of cases.

In Chapter 4, we saw how Joe's work with Suzy helped to develop his instructional knowledge and skills in supporting students' writing. As the story suggests, there came a point when Suzy and Joe judged that working with ISA's literacy coach, Phyllis Tashlik, would support Joe's continued development. Suzy relates, "Phyllis has deeper expertise than me in inquiry and a huge breadth of curricular knowledge." In addition, as Joe and Suzy's work on schoolwide issues crowded out time to focus on instruction, Suzy recognized the value of a coaching relationship for Joe that would do just that.

During her first several years at the school, Suzy had also worked with science teacher Liz Lauben. When ISA added a science content coach, Marc Siciliano, Suzy saw an opportunity for making a connection that would support Liz:

> Liz and I worked together on ways to organize her class and design
> little investigations for students, but she craved content knowledge—
> the particulars of looking at and discussing the content—in ways that
> exceeded what I know. With the sustainable living curriculum, he
> provided that curricular knowledge that allowed her to fundamentally
> change her instruction. I primed the wall, Liz and Marc repainted it.

Making connections with outside resources is not limited to supporting teachers in their instruction. In Chapter 7, we will see some of the ways the coach seeks to connect leaders—both administrators and emerging teacher leaders—with the resources they need to develop and provide others the support necessary for a thriving professional community.

Coaching Habits Examined

A new coaching habit is introduced above: *recycling*. There is no reason to reinvent the wheel with every new classroom assignment or project, especially given limited time provided for planning. Therefore, Suzy says, "I'm a big believer in recycling." Recycling has value beyond its sheer practicality: Helping teachers to see one another as creators of curriculum and experts in particular instructional approaches also grows the professional community within the school, a topic we explore in detail in the next chapter.

CHAPTER 6

Expanding
Professional Community

From the beginning, Suzy's coaching goals at Park East envisioned the development of a professional community in which teachers collaboratively developed curriculum and instruction, shared resources, gave one another feedback, and supported one another's teaching and growth as teachers. She had experienced such a community in her teaching at University Heights High School in the Bronx when Nancy Mohr was principal.

For Suzy, three aspects of that experience in particular stand out:

1. Instructional teams in which teachers "collaboratively work together to build curriculum, engage in each other's classrooms, and develop teaching practices together"
2. Leadership and supervision "fully centered on instruction," with an emphasis on learning about teaching and getting better as a teacher
3. Professional development as "a community of professionals constantly seeking to better the craft through sharing practices and ideas—not about 'improving' individual teachers"

Research on school change has increasingly pointed to the importance of professional community in supporting authentic student achievement. For instance, a study of schools in Chicago conducted by Sebring and colleagues (2006) demonstrates that a strong school-based professional community, along with strong leadership, challenging instruction, and school–community ties, leads to improved student outcomes, including "enhanced student engagement and expanded academic learning" (p. 13).

According to Stevens and Kahne (2006), who also studied small high schools in Chicago, three elements contribute to strong professional communities in schools:

1. High levels of collaboration among teachers
2. Ongoing reflective dialogue about instructional practices and student learning
3. Collective responsibility for student and teacher growth

In Chapter 2, we described Park East as a school that entirely lacked these critical elements: Teachers operated almost entirely in isolation from one another; there were no formal opportunities for reflective dialogue; and there was little accountability either for students' achievement or teachers' development. Joe describes the situation at the school at that time:

> There were very few master teachers. But maybe even more significant than that was the fact that teachers came to school, went to their classes, had conversations outside of the classroom—but always kind of purely social, and even for the most part not even that. . . . There wasn't a lot of sharing of ideas.

Developing professional community is particularly challenging in high schools, in which teaching schedules leave little time to meet with colleagues and teachers typically view their instructional practice as private (Little, 1990). Challenging these organizational norms takes time and sustained effort. In a study of a group of teachers from two departments from a high school who met monthly over the course of 3 years to develop interdisciplinary curriculum, Grossman, Wineburg, and Woolworth (2001) described a trajectory for the development of teacher professional community that begins with the formation of group identity and norms, proceeds through "navigating fault lines"—differences of identity, disciplinary background, and perspective—to eventually assuming communal responsibility for individual growth.

In this chapter, we share four stories that portray the gradual development of professional community at Park East, and the role that coaching played in that development. The stories focus on different contexts within teachers' professional lives:

* A meeting of the faculty-led Professional Development committee provides an opportunity for a young teacher to share her work with colleagues and develop as a leader within the school.
* A department reflects on its instructional beliefs and identifies ways

to support one another's development within a whole-staff professional development session.

- A professional development focus on teaching writing lays the groundwork for a school culture in which teachers share and reflect on their work with colleagues.
- A teacher develops her facilitative leadership skills within a Student Life committee meeting, planning and debriefing a schoolwide event.

Following each story, we distill some of the key coaching habits that help to foster a strong professional community.

WHAT'S IN A LOOK?

This vignette comes from a weekly sixth period meeting of the Professional Development committee. In Chapter 2, we described how the PD committee was formed as a teacher-led vehicle to develop and facilitate schoolwide staff development opportunities.

> Suzy and Jennie, then in her first year as a social studies teacher, are already in the room, having just finished their weekly meeting planning curriculum for Jennie's Economics class. By 12:10 most of the other committee members, three more teachers and the school's math coach, are settled around the table.
>
> Drew, an English teacher and committee co-chair with Joe, begins the meeting by raising the issue of members' attendance at meetings. Suzy suggests that a list of members present be kept and go out in the e-mail with the meeting notes to the full faculty. Drew shifts to the major agenda item for the meeting, nailing down the professional development activities for upcoming whole-faculty PD meetings the committee plans and facilitates. He suggests the PD sessions focus on "instructional problems."
>
> Dave Arthur, a veteran art and science teacher, describes the benefit of seeing a master teacher teach in learning how to manage a classroom, something he had experienced at a professional conference some years before.
>
> Sensing a possible misunderstanding, Drew clarifies: "When I said 'problems' I meant problems about instruction—not 'I have that kid that won't shut up.'"
>
> Suzy, who has been listening intently, jumps in: "Ideally around a goal, for example, 'I want to teach Chinese art. How can I organize the class, think about content? What are the big issues here?'" She pointed out that the "instructional lenses," a framework for guiding peer

observations developed by the ISA leadership coach, which the school had used in "walkthroughs" as a way to articulate instructional goals, had "fallen by the wayside" (see Chapter 2).

Coaching Habits:
▶ Clarifying goals
▶ Using tools

Drew suggests that teachers might choose to "connect to the lenses on their own," for example, getting feedback on a literacy activity they have taught or plan to teach. This sparks discussion of an idea introduced at an earlier meeting, that the next whole-faculty PD session be conducted within small groups; in each one a teacher would present an instructional problem related to their classroom and, using a facilitated protocol, get feedback from the other teachers in their group. The idea generates interest around the table, and the committee considers how the groups will be composed (one presentation within each subject-area team or combining two teams for one presentation) and how the presenters will be identified.

Suzy suggests, "We could do our usual: volunteer people and go sign them up." The strategy is familiar to the committee members, who nod their agreement. "By next meeting, let's ID the people and hit them up."

The discussion moves from deciding how groups should be composed, with the decision made to keep departments together, to who should be "volunteered" as presenters. At this point, Suzy turns to Jennie sitting beside her with a glance of hopeful expectation, and during the brief pause in conversation that ensues, Jennie says, "Sure."

Suzy says, to Jennie and the committee, "We could do any [of what] we talked about today, Nickel and Dimed, writing in economics. . . . "

Drew, picking up on a slight hesitancy on Jennie's part about presenting to her colleagues, tells her, "It's really good. You just put out an idea and hear people talk."

Coaching Habits:
▶ Nailing down the details
▶ Making connections, sharing practices
▶ Sharing enthusiasm

With one presenter signed up, the group moved on to decide about other presenters and the groupings, and review the Consultancy protocol they will use. Drew finds the protocol steps in *The Power of Protocols* (McDonald et al., 2007), and Dave volunteers to make copies for the facilitators to review in preparation for their role.

Coaching Habits Examined

Asked about this episode later, Suzy said, "Those are my favorite moments of the whole job. . . . That's it in a nutshell. That to me is professional community; that's what I feel like I'm trying to help build in the school." The vignette illustrates some of the coaching habits that seek to develop that professional community.

Clarifying Goals. Early in the meeting, Drew suggests focusing the upcoming PD sessions on instructional problems, a goal that resonates with the work of all professional learning communities. Suzy is quick to push the committee to think about what it means by problems and specify the instructional goals teachers are pushing for. In doing so, she recognizes how easy it is for teachers to engage in discussions about their practice that deal mainly with techniques ("Try this . . . " or "I usually start by . . . ") in the absence of clearly specifying the instructional rationale for teaching the content or doing the activity.

Sharing Enthusiasm. As we portrayed in Jennie's story in Chapter 4, Suzy had been working with Jennie to develop curriculum for an economics course she would be teaching for the first time. Over the course of the semester, Jennie and Suzy had developed several activities for the course, and had just begun to plan introducing a complete book into the curriculum, Barbara Ehrenreich's (2001) *Nickel and Dimed*. This would be the first time Jennie taught a "real book," rather than textbook chapters. Suzy viewed the emerging plan for teachers to present their curriculum in the upcoming PD session as an opportunity for Jennie's professional growth:

> I was also thinking it would be a good experience for her to step forward. And I think she's ready to do it, she's ready to hear from people, she's ready to put herself out there. The opportunity has arisen, I know where she is, and I can say, I know she'll do it if I put her forward.

In encouraging Jennie to present—supporting her to step outside her comfort zone—Suzy had in mind the benefits both of Jennie getting her colleagues' feedback and of building up the numbers of people who "publicly put themselves forward to get feedback on their work. The more people who do this at the school, the greater the extent of professional community." Jennie knew Suzy well enough to recognize her motivations at the time. Reflecting on the moment later, she said of herself:

I think it's definitely easier for me to be kind of quiet and stay quiet. I can be a leader, but oftentimes I'm not a natural leader. I think that I was glad to do this because it was a way for me to be involved. Oftentimes, especially in whole-staff PD meetings, there haven't been many opportunities where I spoke out a whole lot. So I think especially because Suzy and I had just talked about that . . . I was actually kind of glad. I thought it was the perfect day for it.

Making Connections, Sharing Strengths. In her coaching, Suzy has strongly supported using tools and structures that allow teachers to see one another's work, for example, the walkthroughs for observing one another's classrooms and various protocols for sharing and getting feedback on instructional plans we described in Chapter 2. In the PD committee meeting, Suzy recognized that Jennie's challenges in planning how to teach *Nickel and Dimed*, and how she was meeting them, could be relevant and useful for other teachers in the school.

In encouraging Jennie to step forward, she weighed some of the advantages and potential pitfalls in making a teacher's work public, including their accessibility to teachers in other disciplines:

We go to the meeting and there's this idea that's coming around, let's have teachers put their heads together to plan something. And it seemed like, gee, this is the perfect thing for some other group of people to give some feedback on: It's accessible content, you don't have to be an expert in econ to give somebody advice on how to teach this book. It's also a book that many people in the school have read.

INTELLECTUALLY ENGAGED

In this vignette, we describe a conversation among the social studies department that occurred during a schoolwide professional development session in order to show what a developing professional community looks and sounds like.

The faculty is gathered for a first-period professional development session planned by Kevin, the principal, now in his second year at the school. Teachers are seated at tables more or less by department. Suzy is sitting with the social studies department, which includes Joe, Jennie, Brianne Tafuro, and Dave Arthur, who teaches an art history class. Ed Poli, just returning to Park East after a two-year absence, also sits with the social studies teachers. Before the meeting gets under way, Suzy makes a quick introduction of Ed and Brianne, telling Ed about the great things she has done with poster projects in her class and suggesting he might work with her in integrating technology on an upcoming project (see Chapter 5).

Coaching Habit:
▶ Making connections, sharing strengths

Kevin begins by welcoming the faculty and talking about his hope that the session will encourage the faculty to "return to thinking about implementing inquiry-based instruction," one of the goals he has had for the school since becoming principal the previous year. He tells the faculty, "I'm not sure we're all that much further along in terms of how you do that." He passes out two documents as resources for a discussion of inquiry, both developed by the ISA: a one-page definition and a multipage implementation rubric designed for school self-assessment and planning purposes.

Kevin asks each department to spend about 20 minutes discussing the question, "What is inquiry supposed to look like in your department?" He directs the staff to five related questions on chart paper at the front of the room and passed out as a handout:

- What is inquiry?
- What should inquiry look like in your department/discipline?
- What are the best learning behaviors that students should practice in inquiry classrooms?
- How can we as teachers change instruction to ensure that learning is happening in an inquiry classroom?
- What inquiry-based practices will you choose to focus on this month in your department?

"By the end of the session, I hope you commit to doing something to help get there." As groups turn inward to begin talking, he adds, "As incentive, Karen [assistant principal] and I want to come around and observe your classes."

Joe, as the senior teacher in the social studies department and thus department head, asks if anyone would be willing to take notes, and Jennie volunteers: "It will keep me focused." He asks the group if they want to work through the questions in a "linear fashion," and Suzy suggests narrowing down their discussion to just three questions. She proposes as most relevant:

- What should inquiry look like in your department/discipline?
- What are the best learning behaviors that students should practice in inquiry classrooms?
- What inquiry-based practices will you choose to focus on this month in your department?

The group accepts her suggestion, and Joe offers a question to get the discussion going: "Let's take a step back, rather than talk about 'inquiry,' what would 'engaged learning' look like?"

Brianne: "They're participating in discussions."

Jennie: "Using evidence."

Suzy, referring to an article from a professional journal Kevin had given to the staff as preparation for the meeting: "As Jackie Ancess (2004) talked about in the article, they're asking big questions. . . . The questions they were asking in [the classroom portrayed in the article] about Lincoln and the Civil War reminded me of Jennie's questions after the kids watched *Primary Colors*."

Coaching Habits:
▶ Nailing down the details
▶ Making connections, sharing strengths

The discussion about what "engaged learning" in the classroom looks like continues for a few minutes. Joe suggests they move on to the second question they had selected about student behaviors: "Anybody have any problem with me replacing 'inquiry' with 'engaged learning'?"

Suzy interjects, "Can we say 'intellectually engaged,' instead of [engaged] in a rote way?"

Dave Arthur asks, "What's wrong with rote?" He goes to describe a lesson he will be doing with his students later that day. "I'm going to ask them if we in the U.S. are more like Romans or more like Greeks." He points out that to answer it, students will need to know some facts about the Romans and the Greeks, which requires, in his view, some rote learning.

Joe asks, "Are you going to give them materials?"

Dave: "No, but you think I should?"

Joe suggests cutting out "a few images" from magazines of contemporary life in the United States to use with his students.

Suzy: "That could be a great sort activity . . . "

Coaching Habits:
▶ Framing questions
▶ Sharing enthusiasm

Joe suggests that if Dave simply asks them to respond to his question without materials, he will get a "very stereotypical response" from them.

In the next few minutes, Suzy and Joe brainstorm with Dave an activity students could do with magazine cutouts on "the idealized Roman/Greek."

At this point, Jennie jumps in to bring the group back to task: "Well, we just sort of skipped to [our] Question 3 . . . "

Joe: "Routines that foster this kind of engagement?"

Jennie: "Journal writing, book-based questions . . . "

The conversation continues in this vein for a few minutes. Joe raises the issue of whether this kind of learning is really feasible without certain structural conditions, for example, reasonable class size, a librarian in the school (which they do not have at Park East), easy access to a photocopier, and so on. Other teachers nod in agreement.

Jennie brings them back to task by saying: "We can't change the structural issues, can we skip to [our last] question and think of practical ways?" Joe suggests visiting one another's classrooms. Suzy adds, "You're at a place where you pretty much know what's going on in each other's classes, more than most teachers." She suggests the visits be planned for when something special is going on that the visiting teacher can learn from, for example, the way Joe uses films, periodically pausing to explain and check on student comprehension, or how Brianne has her students develop posters on assigned topics.

Coaching Habit:
▶ Making connections, sharing strengths

After adding 5 minutes to wrap up, Kevin asks the groups to report out to the whole faculty: "Who can give me a sense of what you're working on?" After several other departments give brief summaries, Jennie reports for the social studies group: "We decided we're going to look at one another's classes, see what's going on, around certain products, for example, how to lead a sustained discussion."

Kevin responds, "Good, next group?" And the discussion and sharing continue . . .

Coaching Habits Examined

In the social studies department's discussion from the PD meeting, we see evidence of a developing professional community, especially in terms of the dialogue about instructional goals and student learning and sharing of instructional practices. Some of the coaching habits that support this developing community are described below.

Framing Questions. When Joe suggests the group use the term "engaged learning" for "inquiry," Suzy asks if "intellectually" can be appended to "engaged learning." As we saw above, in connecting Jennie's questions to those cited in the research article, Suzy brings to her coaching a respect for teaching as intellectual as well as very practical work, and a drive to support other teachers to see it and engage in it as intellectual work. Reframing the question about students' learning here serves to reframe the nature of the teachers' own work. Suzy and Joe's exchange about the term leads Dave Arthur to raise an important question about the kinds of knowledge—rote or intellectually engaged—the students of Park East need, which suggests the kind of "ongoing reflective dialog" Stevens and Kahne (2006) associate with a healthy professional learning community.

Making Connections, Sharing Strengths. There are several points in the meeting where Suzy connects one teacher with another, or with resources. Even before the meeting begins, she introduces Ed to Brianne and suggests that Ed could be a good resource to help Brianne go further with poster projects by integrating technology, and later how other teachers might learn from Joe's use of video in class discussions. She also makes an explicit connection between a point in a professional journal article about inquiry questions to the questions Jennie has been developing for her students related to the film *Primary Colors.* This connection serves not only to validate Jennie's work, but also to close the gap teachers often feel between research on teaching and their own teaching practice—as Suzy says, showing how this research "relates to me."

It is Jennie who pushes the group toward specifying some concrete, doable actions the department can agree on—a hallmark of Suzy's coaching. And it is Joe who suggests visiting one another's classrooms, reflecting Suzy's encouragement of teachers to make their practice more visible to one another. Suzy builds on Joe's idea by suggesting the visits be deliberate and focused, that is, that a teacher plan to visit when he or she might learn from a specific activity or pedagogical approach being used by the host teacher.

PROTOCOLS IN PROFESSIONAL COMMUNITY

The first year of Suzy's coaching at Park East was also the first year ISA asked partner schools to administer writing and math performance assessments to provide the schools with data to inform instructional improve-ment. The system for scoring the writing assessments brought teachers and ISA coaches together for scoring conferences, in which participants worked in small groups to analyze the writing prompt students were given, review the scoring rubric, and then score sample papers using the rubric. Through sharing their scores and the rationales behind them, par-ticipants learned to use rubrics to assess student writing reliably.

Suzy recognized the scoring conferences as an opportunity to intro-duce Park East teachers to the strategy of using protocols, or structured conversations, to examine and reflect on student work—and eventually, teachers' own work. She encouraged the principal to send teachers with her to each of the two scoring conferences held that year (and in subse-quent years). The teachers liked the process and reported back during the school's whole-faculty professional development sessions.

Coaching Habits:
▶ Using tools

The timing was excellent. Suzy and the newly formed PD committee had been looking for ways to help the whole faculty meet the established schoolwide goal of supporting literacy across the curriculum. In commit-tee meetings, they already agreed that finding a way to have faculty share both their writing assignments and their students' work would be a powerful way of enhancing how literacy was supported in all the subject areas. Still, this would be a daunting undertaking in a school in which faculty members had never shared assignments and student work sam-ples from their own classrooms. Suzy asked, "Could we adapt the scoring conference protocol to help the whole faculty gain experience in examin-ing and evaluating student writing?" If so, she reasoned, this could serve as an initial step toward eventually sharing and giving feedback on one another's assignments.

The committee had two important assets to work with: The weekly 50-minute whole-faculty professional development session would pro-vide them with the time they needed to try out the modified scoring con-ference, and the teachers who had already been through a scoring confer-ence could serve as facilitators. The committee knew it was too early to ask any teacher to put their own work or their students' work "out there" for public scrutiny, so Suzy obtained samples from the Park East students' work from the fall ISA writing assessment; within the sample were papers scored at different levels on the ISA rubric.

In January, at a whole-faculty professional development session, teachers read the prompt for the ISA writing assessment, which instructed students to write a persuasive letter to the district superintendent arguing for or against lengthening the school year. Then teachers brainstormed what a "high-quality" student response would look like, and familiarized themselves with the scoring rubric, which included a holistic score from "insufficient" to "skillful," as well as dimensional scores on main point, support, organization, language use/style, and conventions.

The remainder of the session was spent in small groups facilitated by Suzy and teachers who had been to the ISA scoring conferences. Teachers read and scored the three papers, then discussed how they had each scored them according to the rubric. In the group discussions that followed, teachers identified strengths in the student writing but also significant weaknesses. The teachers agreed that for the most part students were able to identify a clear main point and write competently with relatively few errors. In general, they were surprised that writing mechanics did not pose as much of a problem as they had expected. However, only rarely were students able to elaborate on arguments or deploy evidence in support of a position they had taken.

The PD committee planned two follow-up sessions for February. In one, teachers discussed different ways of giving feedback to students on their writing, including using rubrics, editing marks, model papers, and narrative comments from teachers. They discussed how such strategies might be employed to support the students whose papers they had read in the previous session.

In the second session, teachers met in subject departments to discuss the writing opportunities they provided for students within their individual classes. To prime the pump, Suzy and the PD committee had created a long list of possible writing activities—from lists and recipes to oral histories and poems to research papers. They identified those they had already used as well as some they might try. Teacher facilitators from the PD committee asked the teachers to consider presenting both an assignment that included writing and the student work done in response to the assignment at a future professional development meeting.

For the next PD session, the committee, with Suzy's strong encouragement, decided to take the step of having the faculty look at and give feedback on a teacher's assignment and the student writing that it generated. They decided that the Tuning Protocol, a protocol that asks for "warm" (affirming) and "cool" (questioning) feedback on the assignment and student work would provide a good introduction to this kind of work (Allen & Blythe, 2004; McDonald et al., 2007). The committee asked Lisa Purcell, a social studies teacher, to present a research project on world religions. Suzy knew Lisa had a good project and would be willing to present. She also judged that Lisa "could handle it if things got hairy." She asked David Allen to facilitate.

Coaching Habits:
▶ Making connections, sharing strengths
▶ Using tools

During the PD meeting, David reviewed the steps and norms of the protocol with the faculty. Then Lisa described the assignment she had given to students and the rubric she had used to assess their work. The assignment asked students to choose a world religion from a list provided, study it in depth, and interview a person from that religion. Finally, she shared several samples of the students' research papers. The focusing question for the feedback was how to best scaffold the research and writing process.

For most of the teachers at Park East, this Tuning Protocol served as their introduction to using a protocol to look at a colleague's assignment and student work samples and offer critical feedback. As such, there was a hesitation on the part of the teachers to "criticize" a fellow teacher. Even so, the protocol underlined some of the ways Lisa's assignment supported the students to complete the assignment. One teacher even commented that this was the best writing she had seen from Park East students.

In written evaluations and informal comments, most teachers gave the professional development session high marks: "Brave" and "ambitious," they wrote. Overall, the teachers appreciated the relatively in-depth look into the thinking behind the creation and careful execution of a writing assignment the session provided. They were impressed by Lisa's willingness to make her and her students' work public and expressed strong interest in doing this kind of professional development again.

The "Park East Protocol" Debuts

The PD committee agreed that this form of professional development should continue; now the question became, how could the work expand so that more teachers could present their assignments and get feedback from colleagues, given the limited amount of time dedicated to whole-faculty professional development? In collaboration with the Professional Development committee, Suzy developed the "Park East Protocol," an adaptation of the Tuning Protocol that could be completed in about 20 minutes, which would allow three teachers to present in an hourlong professional development session (see Figure 6.1).

In the first professional development session in which the new Park East Protocol was used, three teachers or pairs from math, social studies, and health education presented assignments and samples of student writing. The PD committee had designed the agenda so that all teachers

Figure 6.1. Park East Protocol (2003/04; approx. 20 minutes)

1. Presenter intros what they did, what they hoped to accomplish and how it went. Poses focusing question if they have a burning one, otherwise asks for general feedback/thinking

2. BRIEF clarifying questions (don't get hung up here)

3. Quiet reading of the assignment and one example of student work

4. Small group members give WARM feedback about what they appreciated about the work, what was particularly interesting or strong, etc. . . .

5. Small group members give COOL feedback, i.e.: what lingering questions do you have, additional ideas/suggestions etc. . . .

6. PRESENTER IS SILENT DURING FEEDBACK TIME

7. Presenter reflects on what they've heard, what sounded useful, provoked their thinking etc. . . . presenters respond only to the feedback they want to respond to. (They drive this boat.)

who were not presenting in one of the 20-minute blocks would rotate as a group, enabling each group to experience each of the three presentations during the three blocks. Members of the committee facilitated the small groups. Suzy reminded the teachers that they would have to "tightly facilitate" if each group was going to be able to participate in three rounds. Suzy called "time" between rounds.

Despite the somewhat breakneck pace, teachers commented in their written evaluations that they valued the opportunity to see "live" examples of assignments being used in different classrooms in the school. To some the frenetic pace made the endeavor feel safe because there was not much time to delve into extensive commentary on the quality of the teachers' work. It was viewed by teachers as an introduction to the kinds of writing assignments currently being used as well as an opportunity to provide quick feedback to the teacher.

Coaching Habits:
▶ Inviting feedback
▶ Debriefing

Based on the success of the trial run for the Park East Protocol, the three-protocol format was repeated in the following professional development session with three more teachers presenting and getting feedback from colleagues. At the end of the school year, as teachers formally debriefed the sessions that the Professional Development committee had organized over course of the year, those using the Park East Protocol were mentioned repeatedly as the year's most interesting and worthwhile sessions for their practicality and for the opportunity to discuss the quality of student writing the sessions provided. Some teachers began to adopt and adapt one another's instructional practices, for example, "word walls" and "accountable talk" prompts for discussions.

Reaching a Bigger Slice of the School

In the following school year, protocols became a regular feature in weekly professional development meetings. Through this gradually expanding use of protocols, nearly half the teachers presented their own assignments and student work from their own classes and received feedback from colleagues. One teacher wrote on the evaluation sheet for one of these sessions:

> Even though we've done this many times before, every time we do one of these, I am impressed by how useful they [the protocols] are. Today . . . I saw what was possible in terms of high quality student writing and learned about a new way to get them there. Pretty good.

Reflecting on the positive feedback they gathered from the professional development sessions, the PD committee continued to identify ways to incorporate looking at student work into the school's professional development and expand the scope of the work to include more teachers.

More recent PD sessions have incorporated use of the Slice protocol, in which teacher and student work from across the school on a specified day or during a specified period is collected and displayed (McDonald et al., 2007). In the first Slice, groups of teachers examined the artifacts guided by the focusing question, "Where do we see evidence of college preparatory work?" A second Slice focused exclusively on work done by seniors in all their classes—and was linked to a panel of Park East graduates discussing how they had been prepared at the school for the kinds of work they were now doing in college.

Reflections on Protocols

Suzy identifies a number of reasons the faculty has become "devoted" to protocols:

On an organizational level they've helped us have hard discussions because the structures check random going off and keep people focused on the task at hand. They also model good instruction: there's a plan, it's timed out to work within the limitations of time that always exist, you plan to do what you can do, nothing more; you repeat protocols, tweaking to fit particular circumstances, but the way you use them is to repeat and you get better and better at them as time goes on.

Sharing work and teacher assignments is fundamentally a risky business: It is personal and gets at the core of what teachers do, most often in deep privacy. Protocols create a safe space in which to share our practices; and they usually, in our experience, ensure useful and useable feedback to the teacher.

Protocols have allowed us to talk publicly about instruction in "a think through it mode" rather than "this is all you have do to make this a perfect project/assignment," which is the tenor of typical advice/improvement sessions. We now have shared instructional goals and we can see them play out in real practice because people are willing to and in the habit of sharing their teaching practices and working to improve them, and borrow from each other to make their lives easier and to up the ante instruction-wise at our school.

Jennie identifies another benefit of protocols, especially for a new teacher who may feel isolated and cut off from what other teachers do: "They allow us to understand what went on in the presenting teacher's classroom and to get a glimpse of what our students do in a given day or class period. And on a few occasions, when we got to see their products, we were then able to see the accomplishments of our students from another perspective."

Joe points to yet another aspect of protocols, their capacity to scaffold an inclusive and formalized discussion: "An exercise such as the Slice allowed thirty-odd faculty and administrators to look closely at student work and the teacher assignments that prompt student work. Everyone involved in the Slice feels like they have an equal voice in the conversation and therefore an important voice around the issue of moving instruction—in this case toward the goal of college prep [instruction]."

Finally, Alexis recognizes the value of protocols in "allowing my colleagues who really tend to stay silent an opportunity to express their ideas and opinions and limiting the much more vocal people to a minute or two of airtime." She cautions that following the same format—the same one or two protocols—all the time can become "tiresome," and that some variation, along with predictability, is important.

Coaching Habits Examined

The story above lends credence to the findings of Grossman, Wineburg, and Woolworth (2001) that developing professional community is a long-term endeavor. It also highlights the interaction between changing structures, such as how full-faculty professional development sessions are used, and changes in attitudes and perceptions—from a prevalence of privacy to a willingness to open doors and appreciation for what we can learn from one another's practice. Below we highlight three of the coaching habits that help make these kinds of shifts possible.

Using Tools. As we explained in Chapter 2, protocols have become commonly used tools within the school. Suzy recognized the possibility of leveraging a few teachers' experience with the ISA scoring conference protocol to introduce the strategy through the PD committee to the entire Park East faculty. The story also demonstrates that in using tools, in addition to thinking about the timing for introducing the tool, it is important to match the right tool for the purpose. So, for example, when the PD committee decided to devote a staff PD session to looking at teachers' assignments, Suzy designed a protocol that would do that in a structured, quick, and nonthreatening way. It is a mark of the developing nature of the professional community at Park East that the PD committee took the lead in designing and facilitating the Slice protocols described later in the story.

Inviting Feedback. As a member of the PD committee, Suzy has always insisted on the importance of incorporating written evaluations, called "feedback forms," of committee-run PD sessions. The evaluations serve a number of purposes. Certainly, they give the committee useful data in planning future sessions. They also serve a symbolic purpose: By inviting teachers and students (see the Thanksgiving story below) to share their perspective on an activity or event, and taking those perspectives seriously, leaders and committees demonstrate an openness to the ideas and feelings of others and a commitment to creating an inclusive professional community.

Suzy describes the feedback forms as "an important tool in clearly practicing the habit of asking for feedback. They reflect our belief that planning and execution of professional development should reflect what teachers want out of it—feedback offers the quickest way to figure that out. By taking the temperature of the community, they have signaled directly at times that it is time to shift course.

Debriefing. Closely related to inviting feedback, debriefing consists of the interaction that generates and uses that feedback, for example, discussions of what comes back on the feedback forms. One simple way to begin debriefing, whether after a classroom observation (see Chapter 5) or an event such as the Thanksgiving celebration described below, is to ask, "How did it go?"

"TOO MUCH STUFFING"
(ALEXIS)

In this story, Alexis reflects on her work with Suzy as chair of the school's Student Life committee, which plans schoolwide celebrations and events. Alexis's story reminds us that while a professional community is concerned with the nature of intellectual engagement and how to share instructional practices, it may sometimes mean figuring out how to order enough food or who will set up the chairs for a community event.

It was probably the first week of school, and Suzy knew I would already be thinking about our annual Thanksgiving celebration. Since my first Thanksgiving at Park East 5 years ago I had played a role in helping to organize it. As the years went by I began to play a larger role within the Student Life committee (a group of teachers whose purpose was to organize whole-school activities that might not always be focused on academia). At the beginning of my fourth year at Park East, the Student Life committee found itself without a chair.

Day One of the school year for the students is always our committee's first event, so we needed a plan quickly. Suzy looked to me to take the lead for the event, and with Suzy's help I eventually began facilitating the meetings and became the point person for the committee with the administration. Out of the activities the committee plans, Thanksgiving really became my thing. As I rose to "food czar," Suzy was there to keep me sane in the planning process. After 4 years of fairly dysfunctional, chaotic Thanksgiving events in which we fed more and more students each year, I feared this year would be the worst yet. So in September when Suzy said, "Have you thought about Thanksgiving, yet?" My response was, "OF COURSE! We have a ton more freshmen this year! How are we going to fit everyone in the gym?"

Coaching Habit:
▶ Checking in

Planning and Problem-Solving

Event planning would take place every week at our Student Life meetings and my usually few and far between sitdowns with the principal. Suzy, Clancy (another committee member), and I had remembered that the company we ordered the tables from the year before was fairly unreliable, but we decided we'd give them another shot. Suzy called and got quotes on tables and chairs and would ask me weekly if I had checked with the custodians on how many chairs we had in the building. Finally, by the end of October, we had booked the tables and another member had started thinking about how to set them up.

Then in mid-October I had a great thought that I wanted to run by Suzy and the rest of the committee. I thought that if we fed them from the weight room, which is attached to the gym, rather than from the gym itself, we would open much more space in the gym for seating. Suzy liked the idea of serving the students from outside the gym but suggested the lobby because of all the equipment in the weight room. I thought the lobby was not a controlled enough space for food service. Finally, we decided together that it might make perfect sense for students to go directly from their classrooms to the line in the lobby, get food in the weight room, then go into the gym to eat.

Suzy, Clancy, and I created a seating plan, and all that was left was figuring out the necessary amount of food. Here is where I really depended on Suzy, as I became obsessed with how little food I thought we were going to have. It was now the beginning of November and for the most part our Student Life meetings had worked out the logistics of our celebration right down to the ideas for the centerpieces for the tables. Food, on the other hand, was being offered too slowly for my liking and Suzy knew it. We asked the staff to cook for the event, as it is the tradition of the staff to provide a Thanksgiving meal to our Park East family. Through persistent nagging and an extra order from Fresh Direct [supermarket delivery service], we were able to convince enough people to bring in enough food or at least I thought it would be enough to feed 300-plus students and staff.

On the way home while sitting in traffic the day before the event, I called Suzy from the car and asked what she thought about the idea of a survey after dinner to keep the students occupied until everyone was fed and dessert was ready to be served. She loved it, but asked, "What would it include?" We discussed rating the food and the other aspects of the day as well as suggestions for making the day better and future events. I told her that I would type it up and e-mail it to her that night so she could look it over and then she would make changes and I'd print and copy it the next day.

The survey asked the students to rate the food on a scale of one to ten, what food should we have more of, and which food they liked the least. But they were also asked to include ideas for our annual ice skating trip, which was only a month away, as well as what type of event they would like the Student Life committee to plan for the school—an overwhelming response to this question was "a dance."

Coaching Habits:
▶ Problem-solving
▶ Sharing enthusiasm
▶ Inviting feedback

Thanksgiving Day (Park East Style)

November 22 arrived, and I was surprisingly calm. Suzy was even worried how calm I appeared. The day ran so smoothly. We had between 8 and 10 family and friends of Park East staff come to share our Thanksgiving with us and help serve the students. Turkeys were carved well before we served, students moved through the line effortlessly, the number of volunteers was perfect, the students were patient and thankful for our efforts, and best of all, we had plenty of food! I left the event feeling it was the smoothest we had ever tried to pull off.

On the way home that night, I got a phone call from Suzy just checking in to see how I felt about the day and to tell me that she appreciated all my efforts and the efforts of the committee, which was something I never really felt was offered by other staff members after any of our events. I told her I thought the whole day went really well. There were a few aspects that really bothered me, but I wasn't going to let other people's lack of effort ruin how great it went. She asked if I had read the surveys and I told her that there were some suggestions about the food, like there was too much stuffing and not enough mashed potatoes, but they were mostly positive.

Coaching Habits:
▶ Checking in
▶ Sharing enthusiasm

Debriefing Thanksgiving

The following Tuesday was our committee debriefing meeting. I knew Suzy had a list of topics she would want to cover, and for the first time we had a couple of students at the meeting whom I had invited to participate. When the meeting began I told Suzy she wasn't allowed to share until after everyone else said something. She appeared to be a bit thrown by that statement, but I moved on anyway. I had everyone, including the students, share what they felt went well and what we needed to change for next year.

After everyone had said their piece I said to Suzy, "Okay, now it's your turn. What's still on your list?" When the meeting was over I explained to her that I knew she would have a list of successes and improvements and I did not want anyone to feel that they had nothing to contribute because Suzy had already covered all the topics.

That might have been one of the first times that I felt I really had done a good job facilitating a meeting. Suzy has had a lot to do with opening my eyes to be more of a leader, how to delegate responsibility and to still hold onto my own sense of purpose in the process. Before working with Suzy I would have tried to do it all myself and never really listen to others' suggestions on different ways to do something.

In my weekly meetings with Suzy one of the things we focus on is the agenda for the Student Life meetings. She has guided me into clearly stating the agenda for the meeting and sharing it with the group (not just keeping it in my notebook). Suzy's presence at the Student Life meetings also has kept my tendency to digress and cut people off to a minimum. I tend to have a vision of how I want the events to go; thanks to Suzy forcing me to take a step back and reevaluate the ideas others have contributed, we have broadened ourselves just from the "party planners" we had been viewed as by the rest of the faculty.

Coaching Habits:
► Modeling facilitation
► Inviting feedback
► Debriefing

Now I feel much more confident running the meetings when Suzy is not there because I have learned to stick to my agenda, hear everyone's ideas, and table discussions that do not necessarily pertain to upcoming events. Suzy's teaching me the ins and outs of facilitating committee work has led me to be a lot calmer now when I think ahead to next year's event.

Coaching Habits Examined

Alexis herself identifies two ways Suzy as her coach helped her as chair of the committee: "Keeping her sane" and helping her develop facilitation leadership skills. Below we discuss some of the specific coaching habits through which Suzy was able to support Alexis in developing as a leader within the school community.

Checking In. As Alexis assumed the leadership of the Student Life committee, Suzy was diligent about checking in with her to make sure Alexis was thinking ahead to upcoming events and that specific tasks, such as ordering chairs, were being taken care of. Perhaps the most important aspect of checking in is as much emotional as it is practical: checking in on how the group leader is feeling before, during, and after the event.

Modeling Facilitation. In Alexis's facilitation of the committee meeting, we see reflections of many of Suzy's beliefs and practices around facilitating meetings—a critical role in any professional community and one that needs to be played by multiple people—including:

- Making agendas and sticking to them.
- Including as many voices as possible in making decisions (even when it meant asking Suzy to hold onto her list).
- Being able to step back from your own perspective to allow others' ideas to get out onto the table.

Inviting Feedback and Debriefing. These linked habits are critical in expanding ownership of the school's programs and its direction among the faculty—and students. Alexis describes how Suzy influenced her idea of the after-dinner student survey.

> Suzy has always pushed the value of hearing both staff and student opinions. She and I had decided at the beginning of the year to survey the students about the whole-school events to determine which traditions to continue into this year, so I knew that she would think the idea would benefit the committee as well as give the whole student body a chance to offer their ideas for the next Thanksgiving celebration.

Sharing Enthusiasm. Closely related to the habit of checking in is the coach's sincere expression of enthusiasm, for example, for Alexis's idea of the student survey, or for the overall job she did leading the Thanksgiving planning and execution. As Alexis points out, taking on leadership tasks within a school is all too rarely validated or celebrated by one's colleagues. As a coach, Suzy provides teachers with the praise and encouragement many teachers are often quick to offer their students but not necessarily to one another.

In all of the stories, it is possible to see in the behaviors and voices of the teachers many traces of Suzy's approach to coaching, for example, Jennie pushing the social studies group to identify concrete steps to take; Joe opening up a question about the use of the term "inquiry" within the same discussion; or Alexis facilitating the Student Life committee meeting so that everybody would feel welcome to share their perspectives. The goal for the coach is never to reproduce himself or herself in the practitioners with whom he or she works, but rather to be extremely deliberate about what he or she does to model the habits and behaviors of professional community; support others in developing these habits, through checking in and offering feedback; and create space for others to practice these habits. Sometimes, as Alexis observes about herself, this means to take a step back so others can take a step forward.

Of course, the goal of developing a strong professional community is not just to develop facilitation skills or have intellectual conversations about teaching. These must be in service of improved learning opportunities for students. Joe's observations about how the professional climate at Park East has changed illustrates the powerful influence such an improved climate can have for students:

> Now you walk through the building and instruction is at such a
> higher level [than when Suzy arrived]. I think the main reason is
> because people are sharing ideas . . . not as much as we would like,
> but [teachers] are getting to the point where they are comfortable
> with looking to others for help, and it's not just, "Hey, I need
> help with Johnny because he's a pain in the ass," it's how do I
> better develop this assignment, and people are beginning to share
> techniques.

CHAPTER 7

Growing Leadership

As the demand for principals increases, driven in part by the growth in the number of small high schools, there has emerged a renewed focus on leadership and accompanying recognition that principals and other school leaders need support to maximize their and their schools' effectiveness. While Suzy is not a leadership coach—ISA has a leadership coach who works with the growing network of ISA principals in order to support the development of a professional community focused on instructional improvement—she works closely with Park East's principal and other school administrators.

A focus of her work with the administrators is to support them as instructional leaders who set schoolwide goals and priorities for instruction and create the structures and mechanisms to support teachers in developing their instructional skills in light of those goals and priorities. Coaching can play a useful role, in Suzy's words, in "keeping instruction the focus of the school despite the huge pulls for it to be otherwise" and helping leaders "see how other important elements of school life need to reflect the commitment to quality instruction."

As literature on distributed leadership (Elmore, 2000; Spillane, Halverson, & Diamond, 2001) argues, leadership is not limited to principals and assistant principals. In order to create and sustain schoolwide coherence around instructional goals and values, it is necessary for leadership to exist across and deeply within the faculty community, with teachers taking on responsibility for more than their own classrooms. These "indigenous leaders" (Grossman, Wineburg, & Woolworth, 2001) play critical roles in the professional development of their colleagues, the development and facilitation of committees and departments, and the creation of a school culture that models collaboration and dedication to instructional improvement.

Instructional change and distributed leadership are linked. Research by Peggy Sebring and colleagues (Sebring et al., 2006) has demonstrated that strong school-based professional community and strong leadership

113

are two of the critical ingredients for improving student outcomes, including "enhanced student engagement and expanded academic learning" (p. 13).

Early in her work with the school, Suzy and Nick Mazzarella (then principal) recognized that serious instructional improvement would be necessary to move the school from a failing one to a good one, and that such a transformation would require a depth of commitment to professional development across the faculty. Getting teachers to buy in to such a commitment would be impossible in a school in which decisions were made by administrators, and instruction was delivered by teachers behind closed doors—to administrators and one another. Before instruction, or professional development, for that matter, could change, the school's overall decisionmaking processes had to change.

Suzy's view, which would be shared by the principal, was that the school would need to expand decisionmaking across the school by developing teacher leaders from within the faculty. This meant working with the principal and other administrators to make changes in the way organizational decisions were made, and to do so in an inclusive and public manner. The result of these changes, Suzy believed, would be a transformed and energized professional culture in which teachers and administrators took responsibility for the entire school's transformation—as she has said, "to make teachers and teaching practice the heart of the school. When the teaching's good, the school benefits, and the kids benefit."

When Kevin McCarty became principal of Park East, he recognized that Suzy's coaching encompassed supporting teachers' instructional practice, developing and cultivating teachers in leadership roles, and supporting his own development as a leader.

In this chapter, we highlight five strategies that support the development of schoolwide leadership focused on instructional improvement:

- Establishing and maintaining open and ongoing communication with the schools' administrators and faculty.
- Planning professional development and community development events—and doing so in an open and inclusive yet focused manner.
- Scheduling regular faculty meetings, creating agendas, and taking minutes from the meetings and making them public.
- Providing models and tools for facilitating discussions of teaching and learning on a regular basis—and feedback for developing facilitators.
- Creating recognized structures and roles for faculty members to develop and practice real schoolwide leadership—and modeling how these roles are played.

Each of these strategies involves habits that have been introduced earlier in the book. To illustrate each, we return to some of the coaching interactions and teacher stories presented earlier in the book—this time through the lens of leadership development—and introduce several new examples. We conclude with a mini case study demonstrating how the habits come together in coaching leadership.

BECOMING THE CONDUIT FOR COMMUNICATION

Schools are all too often places where teachers and administrators are estranged from, or at least suspicious of, one another. This makes a coach's work fraught with risk. If teachers think the coach is an agent of the principal, privately sharing information or opinions on their teaching, they won't trust him or her; and without trust there is no chance for authentic collaborative relationships to develop, like those described in Chapter 4.

On the other hand, if the coach interacts exclusively with the teachers, with little or no communication about important issues with the administrators, then there is little chance that the coach will be able to work with them to help create conditions for professional community around improving instruction. In that case, the temptation to become "one of the team" (i.e., the teachers) may actually impede the coach's effectiveness in helping to improve conditions for those teachers.

The lack of trust among teachers and administrators (and among teachers) is heightened if not caused by the way decisions are often made in schools: behind closed doors with little or no input from teachers (or input from only a few teachers). Such was the case when Suzy arrived at Park East: in Chapter 2, we described the toxic professional culture she encountered. To take on this culture—and the double bind outlined above—Suzy adopted the role of—and presented herself as—a conduit between the teachers and the administrators who could "raise concerns of the teachers" with the principal and other administrators in ways that did not expose individuals. Suzy describes some of the ways she was able to play this role:

> In my regular weekly meetings [with administrators] I'd bring
> up issues the teachers were concerned about, for instance, having
> schedules distributed at the last minute, shifting students around
> without telling teachers, giving out class lists on the first day of school
> rather than earlier—so that teachers know who is in their classes and
> how many copies to make on the first day! I let the teachers know
> that when I had the chance I'd bring up their concerns to Nick [the
> principal], and then I did so and tried to get things addressed.

The conduit role began to bear fruit, as Suzy describes: "Once a few things did change then they saw that I was serious about raising *their* concerns— if not always getting a change they wanted—and Nick saw that I was reliable in bringing up issues that were brewing before eruption."

Coaching Habits Examined

Certainly the most prominent habit in regard to playing the role of conduit is to maintain *regular and open communication*, with teachers and administrators. In order to do so, the coach must sometimes create opportunities for communication—through *checking in* regularly with people and *inviting feedback* from them. Much of this occurs in informal conversation, but can also be carried out more systematically, for example, with the feedback forms teachers fill out after professional development sessions.

PLANNING (OF COURSE!)

It is often said about schools that what gets measured matters; but one might equally say, what gets planned happens—or has a fighting chance to. Planning, as a coaching habit Suzy practices and models, has come up again and again in this book. In Chapter 4, we identified instructional planning with teachers as the central component of Suzy's coaching; as Joe pointed out, Suzy's dedication to planning may be the "number-one thing" Suzy does as a coach. However, her experience in schools, as well as orientation in life, has only underlined why it is important for leaders to be effective planners. Suzy likens school-level planning to teachers' classroom-level planning:

> We don't want teachers to go to class without a plan, without a
> big idea and a strategy to deliver it, and the same goes here [at the
> organizational level]. Planning is the antidote to the frenetic nature
> of schools. To borrow Michael Fullan's (1993) metaphor, schools are
> usually "fire, fire, fire" kinds of place. They fire away using the latest
> fad. I try to be, "plan, ready, fire, adjust, and fire again and again and
> again." The planning also comes from my belief that deep change
> takes time, commitment, and focus, and the planning is essentially a
> constant focusing and refocusing on the big ideas and goals.

Planning in and of itself does not guarantee change or results; it can become an exercise in marking time. Michael Fullan (2006) points out in his strategies for "turnaround leadership" that "all successful strategies are socially based and action oriented," and recommends "change by doing rather than change by elaborate planning" (p. 44). Throughout, we have seen the emphasis in Suzy's coaching on a socially based decisionmaking process with its emphasis on developing and working through relationships. But how does Fullan's skepticism about planning square with Suzy's emphatic embrace of it? "Quick turnaround," she replies. "The key to me is the word 'elaborate.' . . . I think you have to plan, make calendars, etc., to use time well. I don't think you just plan and plan and plan and create the perfect sculpture; you plan and quickly after that you dive right in."

In observing instances of collaborative planning in which Suzy has been involved, whether it is for the first ISA Summer Institute team time (see Chapter 2) to the PD committee planning for teacher presentations in protocols (see Chapter 6), we see an emphasis on lean, action-oriented planning rather than the elaborate planning processes Fullan warns about. Key elements of the plan are discussed, debated, and decided. While there is no strict protocol Suzy follows, it is possible to identify recurring questions, including: What are the goals for the meeting? Who will facilitate? What other roles need to be filled and how will they be filled? What are the materials? How will different parts of the plan time out? Who will be the point person?

All these questions point toward action. In fact, from an observer's point of view, one of the dominant impressions from the planning sessions Suzy facilitates and, more and more, participates in as others take on the facilitation role, is how quickly they move and how much gets decided and recorded in very little time—the most precious commodity in a school. One of Suzy's oft-repeated questions to a teacher, an administrator, or a group is, "What can we pull off?" The intent is not to limit ambitions but to recognize that within the constraints of time, money, and competing demands, many ambitious plans never lead to any action, while those that push the needle just a little beyond where it reads now can lead to noticeable results. And realizing one small success makes the next one more likely, for teachers and school communities as well as students.

One of the most effective ways Suzy supports planning is how she models it and makes her own planning artifacts public. There is probably no adult in the school who has not sat with Suzy and her ever-present notebook with her daily and weekly schedules and plans, together with assorted Post-its with questions she wants to ask when she sees them.

Coaching Habits Examined

Planning with leaders and developing leaders is supported through helping them to *frame questions* and issues that need to be addressed, *clarify goals, set achievable targets* ("What can we pull off?"), *nail down the details* of the plan (who, what, when, etc.), and regularly *checking in* to encourage and model follow-through.

WHEN CAN WE MEET? WHAT'S THE AGENDA?

There can be no real professional community if its members never or only rarely meet. In Chapter 2, we described how one of the critical moments in Suzy's first year of coaching came with the agreement of Nick and Beth, the ninth-grade team leader, to call a team meeting. Of course, this did not immediately transform either the professional culture or the teaching within the school, but it created a forum to begin discussions of school-wide issues that included the administration and the entire faculty.

The insistence on having agendas for meetings might seem like mere common sense. In school settings, however, meeting structures, whether explicitly or not, often reflect and reinforce the unequal balance of power within the organizational culture: Principals deliver information; faculty members take it in, ignore it, or act out—actively, through questions that are really judgments, or passively, through doing grades or reading a newspaper at a back table.

Creating an agenda serves several purposes: it commits the leader of the meeting to making the issues public and addressing those during the meeting. Once creating and keeping to agendas becomes currency in a school, it becomes possible to use the agenda as a mechanism with which to negotiate how the meeting will be used and which items will be included, issues discussed, and potential decisions made. Through these discussions about the agenda, the power over what is taken up and what is decided begins to be distributed among the faculty. For example, a sample agenda from a September Student Life committee meeting included these items:

- Debrief first day of school.
- Preliminary planning for Halloween.
- How do we encourage students to attend?
- A few ideas regarding Thanksgiving?
- Any other business?

The ritual of following up a meeting with notes or minutes e-mailed or copied and put into faculty mailboxes confronts a perception common in many schools that meetings are pro forma—we have them because somebody, usually the principal, feels we have to have them, but they don't serve any real purpose. The notes serve not only as a reminder of decisions made but as an accountability mechanism: This is what we have committed to, whether that be the principal, AP, or teacher who agrees to chair an ad hoc committee developed during the meeting in response to an issue or problem. Minutes also signal that decisions are being made in the open—Suzy: "no secrets, no surprises." They become an artifact that invites others into the ongoing professional discourse, as we saw in

Chapter 2 with the use of a faculty listserv to post agendas and minutes and discuss schoolwide issues.

Entering that discourse is a first step toward becoming a leader within the professional community. Suzy points out that the minute-writing, which can seem like a housekeeping chore, can be the entry point into a leadership position. "It is often the first step: Your name gets publicly attached to a document that gets mailed to the entire faculty. You begin to practice the habit of [ongoing] communication by asking yourself, will people get what I've written?" Working with new committee chairs or others preparing the minutes, then, becomes an important coaching practice.

Suzy's emphasis on meetings, agendas, and dissemination of minutes or notes was not only intended to break up the negativity of the professional culture of the school but to provide tools for emerging teacher leaders, like Jennie, Joe, and Alexis, to apply in the settings in which they take on leadership roles. Alexis's reflections on the impact of Suzy's coaching on her leadership of the Student Life committee touch on this explicitly: "Now I feel much more confident running the meetings when Suzy is not there because I have learned to stick to my agenda, hear everyone's ideas, and table discussions that do not necessarily pertain to upcoming events."

Coaching Habits Examined

A big part of coaching for professional community, as we have seen, is *pushing for structures that support collaboration*, including meetings—for committees, departments, and other groups, as well as whole-faculty meetings and professional development events. For these meetings to be seen as useful to the participants, it is essential that they be thoughtfully planned and facilitated. Coaching here involves *clarifying goals; modeling the norms of collaboration*, for example, setting and following agendas; *modeling facilitation;* and *inviting* and *reflecting on feedback.*

MINI CASE STUDY: PREPARING FOR THE ISA SUMMER INSTITUTE

Coaching the leadership of others is tricky. It means staying involved without doing it all. This involves a great deal of reminding and asking questions, evident in how Suzy works with the administrators and teacher leaders in planning for the annual ISA Summer Institute.

For the first several years, when the school had few if any habits of collaboration, Suzy had led the planning of the Summer Institute team time, the daily blocks of time for schools to meet and plan. She had worked closely with Nick and Van to construct the agenda for team time, determining

which working groups and other constellations, for example, departments,
would meet and for how long.

By the time the third summer institute rolled around, with functional
committees and departments established, with teacher leaders, Suzy was
able to step back from direct planning into a reminding and questioning
role. She describes four steps of her coaching in this new role. Through each,
her emphasis is on supporting a process that will advance the school's goals
as they relate to instruction, involve the entire community, and make the
best use of time and limited resources.

Getting the ISA Summer Institute on People's Radar Screens

"As May hits," Suzy recounts, "I will raise 'June is around the corner'
at my weekly meetings with principal and AP, asking questions such as,
'When are we going to plan it?' 'Who should be involved in the planning (e.g., Cabinet, PD committee)?' 'What will the planning process look
like?'"

At this point, Suzy reminds the school leaders of the ISA expectation
that "a big part of making the institute useful is people feeling like what
they plan can actually happen. The principal has to think both about the
people who are going, letting them know they are authorized to do things
for the school, and about those who don't attend."

Sketching a Framework

"I make a skeleton schedule for team time, for example, the Summer
Institute gives us four days with 3 to 4 hours per day for team time." The
schedule gives the planners an idea of how much time they have to work
with as well as how the team work time relates to other aspects of the
institute, for example, when team time follows teachers' curriculum sessions. This is important, Suzy believes, "so that what we do as a team
is integrated with ISA sessions on inquiry curriculum. It helps build an
intellectual community: If there's an interesting key idea in one of those
sessions, we can talk about it as a whole faculty."

Listing the Configurations

"I create a list of the configurations of groups that meet, work groups,
committees, departments, etc., and routines we usually do at the SI, for
example, a welcome/initiation event and a closing event. I get that out as
a list. Then leave it to them. Each configuration comes up with goals and
tasks." Suzy describes a set of three questions she asks each group to ad-

dress in their planning: What needs to be done? What needs to be honed (made better)? And what new needs to added?

These questions have proven useful to help each group come up with a list of goals and tasks and how much time they need during the overall team work time, for example, the PD committee might decide it needs 2 hours of team time to assign new teachers "buddies," delineate roles and responsibilities of this position, make a PD calendar for the year, and so on.

Making It Public

"Sometime in mid-June, whoever is coordinating the planning, the principal, AP, or the PD committee chair, gets out a draft of the whole schedule to everybody out on the listserv so that everybody knows [what's happening at the institute]. . . . Every minute of time will be accounted for."

Suzy's coaching around the planning of the institute team time reflects the value she places on planning, openness, and concrete artifacts and products. "Each group will leave with something tangible, hatch a concept, and write it down; for example, make a calendar for PD sessions or Student Life events for the year." The Summer Institute team work time ends with a celebration of the work, and each group presents its plan to the whole group. Suzy reminds the school leaders that it is critically important to involve those people who do not go to the institute in the plans developed there and make sure that they, too, have a role in realizing those plans so that "it's not just thumbs down" to what has been planned by their colleagues.

EXPANDING FACILITATION AND DEVELOPING FACILITATORS

One of the most critical habits for any developing leader, whether a new principal or a teacher chairing a committee, is the ability to move a meeting forward with the creation of a plan that relates to agreed-upon goals and specifies achievable actions in a limited amount of time. Add to that making the planning process inclusive, and you have a tall order for anyone stepping into a school leadership role for the first time.

Planning meetings, creating and following agendas, and reporting back to the faculty are some of the processes Suzy has modeled throughout. Her coaching has also emphasized the development of facilitation skills, especially, as we described in Chapters 2 and 6, through the use of protocols to structure inclusive and productive discussions of important issues, usually ones closely related to instruction.

In *The Power of Protocols, Second Edition*, McDonald et al. (2007) recognize that facilitating protocols is a form of leadership, one they term *facilitative leadership*: "One of the values of using protocols as learning formats, in our view, is that they can accelerate the development of leadership" (p. 13). Protocols provide a relatively safe structure within which to share practice, give one another feedback, and also for teachers and administrators to develop facilitation skills.

Suzy keeps a copy of *The Power of Protocols* with her as she looks for different contexts in which protocols could be useful and support the development of facilitative leadership. In discussions with teachers and administrators, she invites them to play with different protocols for different purposes, telling them that "these protocols are kind of like different lesson plans or ways to structure and organize a class." For example, when the Kevin, the principal, was considering redoing the bell schedule, the Programming committee decided to use a Tuning Protocol for faculty feedback. Some of the other protocols that have been used include Wall Talk and the Consultancy.

On several occasions, Suzy has looked for opportunities to take advantage of external resources, for example, when Suzy, Nick, and several teachers participated in a district Facilitator's Institute (see Chapter 2). Later, Joe and Suzy discussed how to expand the number of people trained in facilitation; along with Kevin, they asked Anthony Conelli, the school's DOE network leader, to lead a few sessions to renew and refresh the school's facilitative leadership and support the new principal in facilitating the Cabinet meetings.

Along with using tools such as protocols, giving feedback is a critical coaching habit. Suzy tries to give feedback to whoever is facilitating the meeting. Her informal feedback to the facilitator works within a wider professional culture of giving and responding to feedback, using feedback forms after every professional development session, staff retreat, and so on. The PD committee has developed a ritual for full faculty meetings of reading back last week's feedback forms "so people would know we take them seriously and do actually read them, and that we can take criticism."

Coaching Habits Examined

The most obvious habits here are *modeling facilitation* and *using tools*, such as protocols. However, it is equally important to notice the coach's role in *checking in* with developing facilitators as well as those who present their work (and their students' work)—about emotional responses as well as practical matters, such as making sure they bring enough copies.

Coaching also models the need to make decisions explicit, that is, *write it down*, so they can be shared, reflected on, and made public. Another habit that is particularly important to model is *inviting feedback* from everybody involved and building in time to *reflect on the feedback*.

GIVING IT STRUCTURE

From her earliest days in the school, Suzy sought out teachers who could become leaders within the professional community she worked to develop. Her first candidate was John Giambalvo, a social studies teacher well respected by his colleagues. In Chapter 2 we tell the story of how their work together helped bring the faculty together to begin to discuss issues of teaching and learning and begin to plan together as a team.

At that time, most of the work John and other emerging leaders did was informal and unofficial. To sustain and enlarge distributed leadership within school setting, however, structures need to be created and roles identified and authorized by the official leadership of the school. In her work with the administrators, Nick and Van, then Kevin and Karen, Suzy continually pushed for creating decision-making bodies—the Professional Development, Student Life, and House committees, the disciplinary departments, and the Cabinet—and identifying teachers to take the lead in each, including many whose work has been described in this book: Alexis, Joe, Jennie, Drew Allsopp, Liz Lauben, John Giambalvo, and Lisa Purcell.

These committees and departments served multiple purposes: They provided forums for important problems to be discussed out in the open; they distributed the decisionmaking authority across the faculty without usurping the bottom-line authority of the principal; they created a time and place for planning and evaluating (collecting and discussing feedback); and they gave new leaders space for trying out and developing their leadership skills. Committees will change and evolve as the school develops, assesses progress, and sets new goals, but the need for structures that are public and authorized to make decisions will remain.

Teacher leaders at Park East take on many tasks that involve leadership outside of committee work. These might include scheduling assessments; coordinating grade-level teams; developing, scoring, and entering data from new formative assessments mandated by the DOE; and organizing schoolwide afterschool activities such as the basketball intramurals. And leadership often takes the form of on-the-spot (or on-the-fly) problem-solving in which two or three teachers, administrators, (and often) the coach do a quick review of the problem to be solved, consider alternatives, and make a plan, for example, when copies of state examination answer booklets needed to be located at the last minute, and Suzy, Joe, and Alexis huddled to figure out who would approach a nearby school for extra copies.

These examples of leadership that is collaborative, distributed, and focused on developing a school culture focused on instruction offer evidence that teachers have taken on ownership for the direction of the school and demonstrated a willingness to put in the effort needed to move in that direction. In this regard, the most significant development in teacher leadership is also the most significant organizational change impacting instruction: having professional development at the school run by the teachers with administrative guidance and support. As Suzy says, this "turns the whole paradigm on its head," turning over the responsibility for change to those who will actually carry it out in their classrooms and with their students.

Coaching Habits Examined

Good coaching, in a sense, is working yourself out of a job by helping develop the capacity of the institution and those inside it to do the things you start out doing. One of the first steps to getting there is *identifying potential teacher leaders*. This no less critical in Stage 3 of coaching than it is in Stage 1, since there will always be turnover in schools and the need for new leaders to jump into the fray. In every stage, *problem-solving* is critical, for example, in identifying and addressing the issues that may be keeping a committee from working well.

Another aspect of the job has to do with working with the leaders to *establish structures* that support collaboration, which will allow, if not guarantee, that the work will continue even as the people change. Perhaps in this more than any other arena of coaching, the habits of *balancing priorities*—between getting something done and supporting others to learn how to do it—and *being flexible* and responsive are called for.

CHAPTER 8

Reflecting on Coaching

Throughout this book, two recurring themes are feedback and reflection. We begin this final chapter by considering some of the ways a coach invites feedback on and reflects on her own coaching. From there, we share a story that illustrates, from a different angle, some of the coaching habits we have described throughout the book—most significantly for our purposes here, *inviting feedback, reflecting systematically,* and *balancing priorities.*

The story serves as a jumping-off point for some concluding reflections on coaching—and some advice for coaches and the teachers and administrators with whom they work—from each of the book's contributors. Among the lessons the stories offer is the importance of the coaching habit of *persisting* in the face of obstacles and initial resistance from the practitioners who will become allies, friends, and collaborators. Finally, we reflect on the value of coaching as a permanent part of a school's makeup.

TURNING INWARD AND REACHING OUTWARD

It may seem difficult to believe, given the remarkable number of interactions Suzy has with school people every week—in person, online, and on the phone—but she has often described coaching as a lonely experience. Because of its unique insider–outsider status, there is no one in a like position within the school to provide feedback, exchange ideas, or just blow off steam. That status may make it more challenging for a coach to get feedback on her own work—something she constantly facilitates for others.

In Chapter 3, Suzy described how she regularly logs her coaching activities and keeps a journal on big-picture elements of her coaching and the school's development. She also seeks out opportunities for feedback from others in a similar role. The monthly ISA coaches meetings provide a structured opportunity to do so, especially after coaches were assigned regular peer groups to meet in. Especially helpful for Suzy in figuring out how best to work with administrators at the school was the chance to learn from coaches like Bill Sigelakis who had deep experience as school leaders themselves.

The ISA coaches meetings also provided another opportunity to make connections that could be exploited for the school: it was in her coaches group that Suzy connected with Phyllis Tashlik, the ISA literacy coach, whom she later matched up to work with teachers at the school (see Chapter 2):

> I'd routinely ask her to review assignments with me or to help me think of good questions or types of questions related to books. She taught me to always think about "author's intent" questions as being linked to the effect of the text on the reader; relationship between two ideas types of questions; and "you can read this book, this way or this way" types of questions. I apply this template all the time in working with teachers.

Not satisfied with the once-a-month opportunity for feedback, Suzy continually reaches out to other people she believes can offer her feedback or serve as a sounding board for something she is working on at the school, including other ISA coaches and staff members, NYC small school principals, and DOE staff members. She is especially eager for skilled, experienced, and thoughtful outsiders to come into the school, observe what is going on there, and share with her and others at the school their perspective and feedback. In fact, the idea for this book grew out of Suzy's eagerness to have David shadow her coaching interactions and discuss with her what he observed and what he thought about it—"warts and all."

The habit of inviting feedback on her coaching practice extends not just to outsiders, but also to those she works with regularly within the school. In the vignette below, we provide one image of how this looks.

"Top 5"

In Chapter 5, we described a regular first-period meeting among Joe, Drew, and Suzy during which they planned their co-taught hmanities course. Our focus then was on the coaching habit of providing teachers with *resources* that may contribute to their planning and instructional practice. Suzy was excited about an article in the *New York Times* about letters to Shakespeare's Juliet left by visitors at a house in Verona—in this case, far more excited about its possibilities for curriculum than either of the teachers.

> With her *Times* nugget rebuffed, Suzy moves on to her to-do list for the meeting: "So for our time today, I'd like to spend about half the

time on Drew's stuff; for the other half, I'd like to pick your brains for my things." The teachers are amenable, and over coffee and breakfast sandwiches, they set to work.

Most of the period-long meeting was involved in planning for an upcoming "BBQ" (book-based question) essay on Orwell's Animal Farm and scheduling the final reading and writing assignments for the year. As the period is coming to a close and the two teachers begin to pack up their materials, Suzy realizes that they may not have time to discuss "her things." She says, "Go, I'll grab you guys later for my issue."

Joe says, "We have two minutes."

Suzy responds, "I just wanted a 'Top 5.' That was Joe's idea, to stress five things I can work on."

In the brief time remaining between classes, Suzy asks the two for input on a short list (or "Top 5") of tasks or activities she should focus on in the remainder of the school year. Joe and Drew agree that planning the remaining professional development sessions should be a priority, along with working with the principal on hiring staff for next year.

Drew says: "I would put hiring at the top of the list in terms of its 'doability' factor." Joe agrees.

They also discuss the merits of focusing on planning for the ISA summer institute rather than devoting time to planning a staff retreat the principal has talked about but has not yet set a firm date for. Suzy takes notes in her ever-present notebook, bracketing some items as possibly less important based on the conversation. When the bell rings to indicate the beginning of the next period Drew and Joe leave; Suzy stays in the room to prepare for her next planning meeting.

Coaching in the Mirror

This brief vignette highlights a number of themes. Certainly one is the coach's openness to feedback on her practice. In an interview, Suzy described the moment at which she asked for a "Top 5" as a request for help in identifying her coaching priorities:

> I was wanting [Joe and Drew's] help in framing what those five things are, things that are big and important but also kind of limited in scope. And because I value [their] opinion, I wanted [them] to help me decide what those things should be.

In reflecting on the Top-5 discussion, Joe also saw Suzy's request for the list as a genuine invitation for feedback on and input into her coaching practices; he commented, "I think she was looking for what her role could be, and this had come out in conversations we had."

Joe also pointed to a quality of reciprocity that has developed within his relationship with Suzy: "We are now at the point—in the past they were kind of Suzy guiding, me listening—where we have some kinds of mutual conversations."

Joe also highlighted the practical aspects of the moment—a habit we have termed *balancing priorities*. In the absence of more clarity from the principal, Joe felt that it would be helpful for Suzy herself to "define five issues that are important to you; that you know you can have an important role in making happen; determine who the people are you need to make those things happen, then what it will look like when you are finished." Joe's idea, which he had raised in an earlier phone conversation with Suzy, was to do something that "often works best for her both in working with individuals and working schoolwide, a practical approach." He came up with the idea for a Top-5 list because "I know Suzy likes to create lists."

This story suggests aspects of Suzy's coaching as if in a mirror. Joe and Drew are enacting coaching practices that they have experienced as the coached teacher: making lists, being concrete, focusing on "doability" (as Drew put it). It also reflects Suzy's commitment to cultivating schoolwide thinkers. Suzy is encouraging Joe and Drew, and other teachers, to take on roles that have to do with schoolwide issues and the deepening of the professional community within the school. Vital to these roles is the ability to support the development of colleagues, as well as their own; in this case, she is asking them to "coach me."

REFLECTING BACKWARD AND FORWARD

At the time of writing of this chapter, it has been over a year since the most recent coaching interactions described in the book took place. The roles of the contributors to the book have changed. Alexis has become the Coordinator of Student Affairs as well as head of the science department. Joe has continued as head of the social studies department and leads a number of the school's initiatives, including the PD committee. At the conclusion of her second year at Park East, Jennie left the school and teaching, at least temporarily (for reasons she recounts below). Suzy accepted the position of part-time assistant principal at Park East, with specific responsibilities for supervision and professional development of teachers. And now Park East has a new ISA coach, Emily Smith.

In this section, each of the contributors reflects on their experience with coaching and what was most significant for them about that experience. They also offer their advice for teachers and administrators who work with (or will work with) a coach—and to new and developing coaches themselves.

Even Teachers Need Coaching (Alexis)

Working with Suzy has allowed me to see the potential teaching experiences the world around us lends itself to. For a new teacher, it can be extremely difficult to identify these "teachable moments"; working with a coach can allow that teacher to develop these opportunities that may seem impossible. Before working with Suzy I never imagined that I would be able to develop an anatomy elective that I would be permitted to teach; now I teach a program of full-year anatomy. Coaches offer a third-party perspective to a teacher's practice that often adds great value to their work. Having worked closely with Suzy for 3 years, we developed both my teaching practice and my leadership skills, which I can now turn around to help guide my department.

I was extremely skeptical about working with Suzy in the beginning because I felt I was being brought into the fold as an afterthought to this new group developing within the school and because I already had a lot on my plate. As a new teacher, it can be incredibly overwhelming to juggle planning, grading, coursework, and mandatory school meetings. Add to that meetings with a coach and it is easy to feel overworked, but the potential it adds eventually pays off. After all the not-so-gentle prodding, I began working with her and it has made me both a better leader and a better teacher. I still have a lot to learn, but working with Suzy sped up the process.

As I reflect upon my work with Suzy, I realize I have also learned valuable tools to help me in my new role as head of the science department. This new role has left me with the responsibility of working with the new teachers in my department, one of whom has struggled to develop meaningful learning opportunities for his students. Recently, I have suggested that he develop a similar human impact project to the water treatment project that I planned with Suzy (see Chapter 4). Rather than testing the water in the building, he would research the use of heating oil and efficiency of the building. In order for him to develop this project, he would need to work with me as well as with the new coach. I have learned that developing projects requires constant updating of timelines, but it is essential to have a general timeline from the beginning.

If asked for by a new coach, the best advice I could give to the coach would be to be both *persistent* and *consistent*. I never would have sought out Suzy to work with her, but she saw the potential leader developing in me and the passion I had for my subject area, and she did not take no for an answer. Whether a coach is entering a school that has never had a coach before or is a new coach for the school, it is important for that coach to realize that sometimes people will be resistant to meetings or planning with the coach: Find a hole in the wall and take it down brick by brick. It may take a while to remove the whole wall (in some cases it may never come down completely), but the product, a mindful way to plan meaningful lessons, will be there in the end.

Administrators need to realize that having a coach in the school can be a benefit to the school community because it will better the practice of the teachers who work with the coach. But it has the potential to be divisive if not introduced properly. Suzy and I started at Park East the same year, and I felt on more than one occasion during that year that there was a special team that worked with Suzy—they were the starters and everyone else was just benchwarmers. As time went on I felt less like a benchwarmer and more like a starter, but then again, Suzy worked with the administration to expand the starting roster. Rather than keep it limited to just those few who were part of the original planning retreat, they worked to bring more of the staff into the fold and not just to replace people who were leaving but to work alongside those original members (see Chapter 2).

I also believe the administration needs to work closely with the coach and keep the lines of communication open to the whole staff on anything that the coach may be involved with that would affect the whole school community, such as the planning of retreats or the annual Thanksgiving celebration coordinated by the Student Life committee (see Chapter 6). If the administration is open to and supportive to the inclusion of a coach into the school community, then coaching can really work.

Stepping Away (Jennie)

After teaching for 2 years, I decided to take a break and try a new profession. This was in large part because I had been in schools for 20 years, as a student, then as a teacher, and was curious about things other than education. After taking a step away for some time, however, I am feeling a continual pull back to teaching. I have maintained my relationship with Suzy, through which she encourages me and affirms me as a teacher—even though I am not teaching now.

Reflection upon my career as a teacher is inevitable as I consider a return to it. Suzy has, without a doubt, been vitally influential in my development as a teacher. She persisted when I was initially resistant by bringing a "menu" of not just suggestions, but helpful supplementing materials. Over time, I was less resistant because I realized that Suzy was not attempting to push an agenda on me, but was truly offering practical suggestions that would both help me develop as a teacher and make my lessons more meaningful to students.

Eventually our relationship came to a point where I was greatly valuing our sessions and setting the agenda myself. Although I still sought her advice, it had transformed into a much more collaborative relationship. This still has effects on me, as the following example shows.

Brianne, the teacher who originally shared my meeting time with Suzy, now teaches Participation in Government, a course I had taught last year. I left behind all of my lesson plans for the course, and Brianne uses some of these. Brianne and I have kept in close touch and e-mail frequently. At one point, this past fall, she was explaining how she was using my lessons on constitutional rights, but was not sure where she would continue the unit beyond what I had planned.

Excited to use my currently dormant creative planning skills, which I developed in large part through my planning with Suzy, I offered to look up and found a variety of articles that dealt with the violations of rights in other countries that would be protected by our own constitutional rights in the United States. Then I developed a set of questions for each article. Brianne and I met to further develop the articles and project. It was extremely satisfying to be in a collaborative relationship once again and planning student lessons the way Suzy and I had worked together.

From Burden to Opportunity (Joe)

I disdain self-reflection. It isn't that I don't see the value in self-reflection, it is simply that I have a really hard time sitting down and questioning my own practice, my motivations, and my actions. Therefore, this last chapter of the book has been very difficult to me to think about. Then it dawned on me that what I would tell a new teacher about working with a coach is:

> In your first year (or three) you will be overwhelmed by everything. If you aren't careful, or already in the practice of self-reflection, you will never take the appropriate time to think about your practice; you won't intellectualize your instruction. You will simply do it without ever stepping back and getting some perspective about what you do. A coach provides that perspective.

I believe a lot of new (and seasoned) teachers worry about their teaching loads and feel that any extra meeting, any new request from the administration, is a burden. Although Alexis, Jennie, and I are very different personalities and our pedagogical and personal philosophies are divergent, one commonality in our narratives is that we all were apprehensive about working with a coach. To paraphrase a conversation with Jennie, the time factor of meeting with the coach, of giving up a prep period for the meetings, created the initial hesitancy to work with Suzy. The expectation—or obligation—that we were to work with the coach was off-putting. In each of our narratives the "burden" of meeting with a coach caused us to flee, hide from, or create excuses not to work with Suzy.

Teaching is overwhelming, but the coach will not create a greater burden. A good coach will lessen the burdens of teaching. Sometimes teachers are the ones who need the education. Simply put, a good coach will help you to be a better teacher. Reflection on practice is vitally important to good teaching, and most of us have a hard time creating the time and space to do it. For the most part the suggestions and conversations teachers have with their supervisors following an observation do not provide an entirely safe space for reflection. If you view the coach as outside the school hierarchy, he or she can be a resource who gives the teacher a safe place to discuss and question their practice.

The coach can help to facilitate the conversations a teacher needs to have about his or her practice—both the inner dialogue of self-reflection conversations and actual person-to-person dialogues that help facilitate productive inner dialogues. As Suzy puts it, the coach can "create a climate of intellectual engagement around instruction." For any teacher beginning a relationship with a coach, my advice is to savor the opportunity. Your collaboration will help you become a better teacher and, perhaps more importantly, a more thoughtful, reflective, and engaged pedagogue.

Advice for an Administrator. My advice for an administrator working with a coach has two parts. First, it mirrors the advice I would give a teacher: Work with a coach because they can provide you with perspective to think about your work running the school that almost no other individual in the system can. Listen to his or her advice; the coach is able to see things that you may not—perhaps because you are so invested in or involved in your own vision for the school. Suzy helped two principals with very divergent personalities identify what was important when they were unable to identify the issues or problems that needed to be dealt with.

Now, when it comes to your relationship to the coach vis-à-vis the faculty, my advice is to allow the coach the freedom to work with teachers with minimal interference from the administration of the school. The coach works best with teachers who see him or her as an ally who is removed from the school hierarchy. This doesn't mean that you shouldn't have contact with the coach about their work with the faculty; it simply means that you should trust the coach, the faculty, and your own leadership to allow the coach and the teacher an autonomous zone were ideas can be shared without continuous involvement of the administration.

Advice for a New Coach. Suzy often refers to herself as an ally of the teachers. She also often repeats her desire to create a climate of intellectual engagement around instruction. My advice is based on these two ideals. Although teachers might be initially hesitant to work with a coach, you are the best ally teachers can have. The more you work to let the faculty know this, the more you help teachers to see you as a resource, a sounding board, a facilitator, and a friend, the quicker you will gain their trust. Once teachers realize that you are an ally and that they can trust you, the more they will seek you out, and the more willing they will be to work with you.

Once you have gained the faculty's trust, a formidable goal of the coach should be to persevere toward making education an intellectual pursuit. Suzy was a catalyst for change at Park East. She was willing to take risks and to push the school to look at teaching as an ever-evolving process. Education to Suzy is a process that required us to open our doors, to converse with one another about important topics, and to share ideas and methods. Park East has undergone a transformation over the past 5 years, none of which would be possible without a coach who saw the potential in the school, its administration, its faculty, and its students. The successful coach has to be able to see the potential in a school when the classroom doors are closed, when the faculty runs away from teaching as intellectually engaged and engaging, and be willing to hold a mirror up to the school and state frankly that here is the place we are and this is what we can become.

Memo to a New Coach (Suzy)

Listen first. Dive in later. Be patient. Plan your time judiciously—and regularly revisit how you plan your time. Think in small, concrete increments. Be humble. Build relationships. Communicate your caring.

By design, coaching is an amorphous role: insider/outsider; theorist/practitioner; doer/facilitator of others; observer/actor. . . . The single best thing a person new to coaching can do is talk to at least two other coaches regularly during their first months on the job. Even better, go visit or get visited yourself and have someone help you set up your routines. That would be my overarching piece of advice: Get coached yourself!

Remember, your most effective coaching strategy is modeling. If you are a real learner and approach all tasks as a diagnostician and learner filled with curiosity, it is easier to bring others into reflective thinking and acting in an intellectually engaged mode, too.

That's the work of a coach in a nutshell: creating the drive and the conditions for school people to be continuous learners and to develop the individual and schoolwide relationships that make it possible. Those who are attuned and honest know that there are no magic bullets in our field. Instead, our work is really about searching for fresh solutions to persistent problems. Doing so demands sparking and stoking intellectual energy in students and colleagues, creating the drive and opportunities for discussion, and learning to continuously address problems in the face of weighty obstacles, including the overwhelming nature of the work, the limited resources, the instability and constant changes, etc.

There's no one way to do this, but there are better ways. The role of the coach is to foster intellectual engagement and commitment to a broader vision that keeps people in schools teaching and leading and part of the field for the long haul—thinking constantly, always moving forward. To do this you, the coach, need to have sustenance and intellectual community as well. Read. Think. Talk. Collaborate. Do.

A PERMANENT ROLE FOR COACHING

The reflections from Alexis, Jennie, Joe, and Suzy provide another set of takes on some of the themes that have run throughout the book: the importance of developing trusting relationships and the recognition that this takes time, effort, and perseverance on both sides—the teacher's (or administrator's) and the coach's; the value of the coach's modeling of practical skills, whether these are in planning projects for students or facilitating a department or committee; the unswerving emphasis on working collaboratively, openly, and inclusively; and the willingness to meet people where they are and help them move forward.

Coaching is rightly considered a capacity-building role, harnessing the unique skills and position of the outsider who works closely with the insiders. However, the accompanying expectation that coaching should be a temporary role within the school—effectively asking coaches to "work themselves out of a job"—in our view does not recognize the essential benefits of coaching.

As the stories we have shared in this chapter and in the book demonstrate, leading a classroom, let alone a school, is demanding, complex, and exhausting, especially for new teachers. In seeking to do the job well, it is natural and predictable that the teachers and administrators lose perspective, develop habits that may be counterproductive to their goals, and slip from manifesting those habits and practices that they know, at least at some level, are necessary and right.

The habits of coaching we have explored in this book are identical to the habits of a healthy, functioning classroom and school as professional community—working through relationships, working deliberately and planfully, working on multiple levels at once, working collaboratively, and working in the open. There will always be a role in schools for someone positioned as insider-outsider and with the skills and experience to do whatever it takes—ask, remind, model, cajole—to support teachers and administrators in developing and enacting these habits. An individual coach will leave eventually, but *coaching* should remain a constant.

One of the paradoxes of Suzy's coaching is that she uses every ounce of her personality to develop in others, and throughout the community, habits that transcend personality. Extraordinary coaches come in all kinds of "personality packages" but will be unified by their tenacious commitment to the growth of the individual teachers and administrators with whom they work, as well as the development of the professional community and school community that those people create and re-create every day.

Afterword

Appendix: The ISA Model

References

About the Authors

Afterword

Seven years ago, when I first began to work as a coach for The Institute of Student Achievement (ISA), our then small group of coaches met monthly with Gerry House, President of ISA, and Jackie Ancess, co-director of NCREST to share our experiences, seek advice from one another, and develop, both individually and collectively, our images of coaching and coaching practices specific to ISA, such as facilitating common planning time team meetings, supporting teachers in planning and implementing instructional strategies that increased inquiry, and planning with counselors to implement distributed counseling.

We had been selected on the basis of our experience and expertise, most of us having been principals of successful small schools. All of us had worked extensively with teachers, and it was expected that we would apply that knowledge to this new role.

Some of us already had done some coaching or mentoring. My first experience was as a teacher–mentor in the mid-1980s when the teachers' union mandated mentoring for first-year teachers. For one year, I worked with a young home economics teacher. During one period each morning, I sat in and observed her class, then met with her over lunch later in the day to discuss the lesson and plan for the next day. That coaching experience, characterized by consistency, continuity, and mutual trust, enriched us both.

The teacher gained some practical classroom strategies, but more importantly, came to understand the value of thoughtful planning and post-lesson analysis. I leaned how to "script" while observing. In doing so, I watched not only what the teacher was doing and saying, but the students as well. Paying attention to everything that was taking place helped me better comprehend the complexity of the classroom and the challenges faced by an inexperienced teacher.

Following my retirement as principal, the Department of Education developed a mentoring program for principals in their first year of running their school. My charge was to assist my "mentees" with whatever issues arose, from budgeting to helping negotiate an unsatisfactory rating for a teacher—the latter being a time consuming, often emotionally draining process of thoroughly documenting the teacher's lessons in a format which is subject to line by line scrutiny in a legal hearing should the teacher decide to challenge the rating.

This experience was most gratifying when the principal was both capable and willing. However, not everyone welcomed mentoring. One principal, seemingly friendly and receptive, nevertheless managed to avoid my assistance for weeks by being constantly "busy." Another, a gifted young woman, told me that she had no idea how I could help her, and implied that she had to "entertain" me during my visits. In these cases, I had to work hard to establish a productive relationship, which I did eventually after losing a lot of valuable time.

Coaching for ISA was considerably more complex, as it involved working with individual teachers, teams, or groups of teachers, as well as the principal. Our coaching goal was to help the school implement the ISA principles with the aim of bringing about positive and greatly improved outcomes for students, specifically graduating college ready, which is ISA's mission.

We encountered many challenges: What were the "entry points" which would enable us to develop relationships with teachers who had not welcomed us with open arms? How might we reach out to a new teacher in need of support who was afraid to expose herself to scrutiny by an outsider? Or a longtime teacher who simply said "No thanks," and locked his door? How to convince the principal who had invited ISA into the school but had no time to meet now that it was important for us to do so? Or, conversely, how could we guide a new principal without encouraging too much dependency? Or help a newly formed teacher team with no experience of collaboration to run effective common planning time team meetings? How could we help teachers to understand and implement inquiry based instruction and assessment? What guidance and resources would help a school to develop an effective advisory program?

Coaching Whole School Change is a book that addresses the challenging work of coaching in all its complexity. Drawn from the work of one coach, Suzy Ort, at Park East High School in New York City, the book provides insight into the coaching role as we observe Suzy persistently and purposefully navigate entry into a school culture which she undertakes to understand—and ultimately helps to change.

Suzy is mindful that coaching in a school with a long history of failing its students and an entrenched professional culture is a transformative process. Because Suzy is in the habit of recording her work in detailed logs, as well as engaging in extensive e-mail conversations online, the book details a rich record of her evolving role. We hear not only from Suzy but teachers who describe their initial reactions to coaching, as well as the eventual impact it has on their teaching practice and roles as teacher leaders within the school.

A skillful coach doesn't approach a teacher with the notion of "fixing" him or her. Even the least experienced teacher is able to talk about what isn't working and can help set the direction in which he would like to grow and develop. When the coach and teacher are in sync, the partnership is energized by their mutual investment in the work.

As an "insider/outsider," Suzy brings a fresh perspective to her work, while at the same time develops important relationships within the school and grows increasingly committed to its progress. During her initial phase of coaching, Suzy learns about the school culture, one in which she finds little evidence of formal collaboration or the structure to support it, emphasis on passing Regents exams, textbook driven lessons, and high student absenteeism. Environments of this kind are more the norm than the exception in our public high schools, and challenge the coaches' ingenuity and determination as they seek to change them.

If change is to take place, a coach needs allies on the faculty, so Suzy slowly developed relationships with teachers and the principal, with whom she found common cause. Over time, she worked simultaneously at multiple levels of coaching by nurturing individual teacher leaders, working with groups of teachers as they gradually emerged to take on important school initiatives, helping teachers to write and strengthen curriculum, working with teachers on daily lessons, and even stepping in to assist with students.

Although this book doesn't present Suzy as a "model," she is an exemplary coach. There are many aspects—or "habits" as they are called here—of coaching portrayed within this book that offer lessons—and inspiration—for other coaches, as well as the teachers and administrators with whom the coaches work. These habits include organizational methods; understanding how to collect and share artifacts; gathering and sharing resources; balancing priorities; touching base with teachers often, sometimes accomplishing much in these brief encounters; putting together groups of teachers with common interests so as to use one's time efficiently; adaptability when encountering unexpected changes in schedule on the day of her visit; acting as a conduit between teachers and the administration without seeming to align one's loyalties with either (or taking sides during internal conflict); and recognizing creativity and cultivating an intellectual approach to teaching. Importantly, Suzy understands what

I too learned as a coach: The job can't be done in just one day a week, so she willingly devotes much of her home time to preparation, e-mail, and telephone conversations to keep her connection to the school active even in her absence.

Thanks to the authors of this book, I've come to think of the coaching not as a temporary, but a permanent element of a school community. Every year, schools absorb inexperienced new teachers. Research tells us that a significant number of them leave the teaching profession within the first 5 years. Schools must find ways to support and sustain new teachers to retain them. A coach may be the most consistent source of support for new teachers that a school can provide. The challenge is how to help schools and districts develop their own capacity for ongoing coaching.

Another important role for the coach is to support teachers in developing projects, units, or lessons by finding resources and making connections, which teachers often have little time to do. Coaches are able to "rove" widely across the entire school, and even among schools and in the community, helping to find resources and make connections which teachers can't easily make for themselves. With the teacher's consent, they may even be a welcomed extra set of hands in the classroom, modeling good practice by example.

In the hectic atmosphere of schools, the coach can "slow down" the frantic pace by offering time to plan, reflect, think about practice, and give helpful feedback. A coach brings experience, expertise, commitment and a fresh perspective. Having walked in the teacher's or principal's shoes (and stayed the course), a coach can be a source of support, encouragement and even inspiration.

Perhaps the one area which is not fully explored in this book, although touched upon, is the frustration a coach feels when the work stalls. Most of the coaches I've known, myself included, are people used to getting things done. Adjusting to a role where your influence is marginal at first, and limited, even over time, can be deeply frustrating. Suzy has the gift of persistence, optimism in the face of obstacles, and the willingness to work in incremental steps. In doing so, the changes she helped to bring about were dramatic, demonstrating how vital a resource to a school an effective coach can be.

Sylvia Rabiner
Institute for Student Achievement

APPENDIX

The ISA Model

The Institute for Student Achievement (ISA) works with high schools and school districts to transform low-performing high schools into successful small schools/small learning communities. ISA believes that in highly-supported small schools/small learning communities, meaningful, sustained relationships develop between teachers and students that facilitate higher student motivation, achievement, and aspirations. ISA's strategic partner in the implementation and documentation of the ISA Model is the National Center for Restructuring Education, Schools, & Teaching (NCREST) at Teachers College, Columbia University.

ISA PRINCIPLES

A clear, explicit set of non-negotiable principles defines the ISA Model. Each school develops a customized plan of how the ISA principles are operationalized in the school's organizational, instructional, counseling, and parent involvement components. Where schools need help in designing a particular component, ISA and NCREST may recommend appropriate pre-packaged programs, curriculum, assessments, organization, and professional development.

All ISA sites implement and accomplish the principles described below. These principles are based on ISA's achieved effectiveness and current educational research. ISA, with NCREST, facilitates the implementation of these principles through the coaching, professional development, and technology strategies that research shows effectively support program development and higher levels of student achievement and school affiliation. The ISA Model principles follow.

1. College Preparatory Instructional Program

The instructional program prepares all students for college admission and completion by focusing on the students' intellectual development and emphasizing the development of higher-order thinking skills, organization skills, habits of work such as perseverance and preparedness, and mastery of basic skills in reading, writing, and mathematics. Literacy and numeracy are embedded in content areas across the curriculum, and students are taught literacy and mathematics skills explicitly where needed. Elements of the instructional program include:

- *An inquiry approach to curriculum and instruction,* focusing on the goal of enabling students to use their minds well (i.e., rigorous intellectual development for all as the central feature of the model). Intellectual rigor in curriculum, instruction, assessment, and student work is based on commonly used criteria for identifying rigor, such as construction of knowledge, disciplined inquiry, and value beyond school.
- *Infrastructure for student support* includes the organizational and instructional structures that provide the academic and social supports necessary for students to successfully engage in an intellectually rigorous, college prep curriculum and produce intellectually rigorous work. Examples include counseling, close and sustained relationships with teachers for the purpose of social and academic development, tutoring, and math and literacy lab classes that provide intensive skills instruction as needed.
- *Development of habits of mind and habits of work,* such as examining phenomena through multiple perspectives and developing time-management skills.
- *Literacy and numeracy across the curriculum.* Opportunities for students to develop literacy and numeracy skills are taught across the content areas; for example, students may examine statistics in social studies and science and do extended writing tasks and exhibitions (oral presentations) across subject areas.
- *Multiple forms of assessment.* The programs use multiple forms of assessment, including performance and formative assessments, standardized tests, and teacher tests to ensure accuracy and equity, guide pedagogical decisions, and help teachers monitor and support student learning.
- *Intensive, 9th–12th grade post-secondary education preparation,* including financial aid guidance, visits to college campuses and other post-secondary institutions, meetings with college admissions officers, parent information, SAT preparation, and courses at local colleges.
- *Internships and community service* from which students can learn about their talents, interests, strengths, and weaknesses in the world of work as well as the demands they will be expected to meet.

2. Dedicated Staff of Teachers and a Counselor

The team provides consistency for students throughout the four years of the program. The team agrees that once students are selected, the team remains committed to their continuance and to their success. Teachers have expertise in the subject area they teach and demonstrate successful experience teaching diverse students at risk. Teachers and counselors value and commit to working collaboratively.

3. Continuous Professional Development

Weekly common meeting time is regularly scheduled for the staff to plan, problem solve, and review student work and progress collaboratively, as a whole and in teams. On an as-needed basis, staff participate in ISA professional development opportunities, such as summer institutes or other professional activities that enhance teachers' content knowledge and pedagogical skills, focuses on diverse learning styles, and integrates instruction and counseling.

The purpose of professional development is to build the capacity of ISA teachers and counselors to develop a program at their school that effectively implements ISA principles so that students achieve at high levels and are adequately prepared for college and the world of work. Professional development has three components: (1) customized training on an as-needed basis; (2) regularly scheduled coaching targeted to program development and strategic planning; and (3) technology.

Customized professional development might include training in pedagogical skills such as instructional strategies for diverse learning styles; content knowledge-building; curriculum development; assessment; strategies for personalization; planning backwards for curriculum alignment with local standards and program and school learning goals; leadership development; planning for the extended day program; parent participation; and creating links to local colleges.

Coaching for program development and strategic planning includes the facilitation of:

- Program planning and implementation: each site builds its program on the strengths of the teachers involved, the interests and needs of the students, and the culture and values of the local context in ways that embody and are consistent with ISA principles and goals. This approach builds local ownership, commitment, and sustainability and is designed to attract intellectually strong, deeply committed, effective, experienced teachers.

- Professional development in organization, curriculum, instruction, assessment, interventions, internships, advisories, student support, and the construction of student post-graduation plans.
- Links to practitioners and schools in other nearby districts, current research findings, and professional development opportunities.
- The development and execution of a process for student recruitment and selection, including the production of student recruitment materials and presentations.
- Collaborative planning, problem solving, sharing of effective practices, and review of students and student work.
- The development of a process for program review, assessment, and revision.
- The identification of expert schools/programs and practitioners, which could serve as resources for new ISA teachers and counselors to learn new practices and organizational structures, do short term residencies, and establish links.
- The development of the family support component.
- Relations among ISA, the school, and the district.

4. Distributed Counseling™

Each team has a counselor who provides direct services to students and their families, sometimes through leveraging available community resources. The counselor works closely with teachers to support the implementation of learning and social interventions for students. The counseling component includes mechanisms such as advisories or family groups led by teachers for the purpose of personalizing the school experience, developing strong student affiliation with the program, and monitoring student progress and achievement. The counseling component also includes initiatives such as peer mediation and conflict resolution to help students develop effective problem-solving skills.

5. Extended School Day and School Year

Goals for students' learning and the school's college prep instructional program drive the length of the school day and year. The extended day and extended school year enable staff to provide students with the time, attention, and other supports necessary for their success with the program's challenging college prep curriculum. The extended timeframe for learning also provides additional opportunities for effective skill and talent development and enrichment.

6. Parent Involvement

Because parental/guardian partnership and support can advance the achievement of children, ISA teams seek parental involvement and feedback with regard to their students' education. Teachers and counselors keep parents informed of students' progress, the development of the program, and its efforts and achievements.

7. Continuous Organizational Improvement

The regular team and faculty meetings provide a forum for continuous organizational improvement and for a focus on accountability for measurable results. Staff use the meetings to self-examine and self-monitor the various interacting components (such as curriculum, instruction, use of time, class organization, professional development, student performance, etc.) to ensure coherence and effectiveness. For an external perspective on program quality, the team participates in a critical friends–type process, whereby a team of like-minded, external stakeholders visits the program to assess its quality of teaching and learning. Staff in network schools can comprise these teams. Additional documentation on program implementation is collected by NCREST and provided to the school for the purposes of informing practice and improving program delivery.

ADDITIONAL COMPONENTS OF THE ISA MODEL

Formative Program Assessment

To assist the team in tracking progress made by students, ISA and NCREST work with schools to implement a Formative Program Assessment, which includes scored samples of student work in writing and math, surveys of students' attitudes and expectations about school and their future, and interviews with cohorts of students.

Team Facilitator

One teacher in the program is the team facilitator, assigned a reduced teaching load appropriate to the coordination responsibilities for the project. The team facilitator coordinates team activities, such as meetings and program development activities. The team facilitator is the liaison to ISA, NCREST, the school principal, and middle schools from which the program will recruit students.

ISA Network

The ISA network provides a forum for cross-site learning, sharing of best practices, knowledge-building, professional development, and the creation of an organizational *esprit de corps*. The network includes activities such as a summer professional development institute, an electronic network for communication across ISA sites, and cross-site visits.

References

Allen, D., & Blythe, T. (2004). *The facilitator's book of questions: Tools for looking together at student and teacher work*. New York: Teachers College Press.

Ancess, J. (2004, September). Snapshots of meaning-making classrooms. *Educational Leadership, 62*(1), 36–41.

Ancess, J., & Gandolfo, D. (2006). *Redesigning high schools: How the Institute for Student Achievement develops and launches new small high schools*. Lake Success, NY: Institute for Student Achievement.

Dewey, J. (1916). *Democracy and education: An introduction to the philosophy of education*. New York: Free Press.

Ehrenreich, B. (2001). *Nickel and dimed: On (not) getting by in America*. New York: Metropolitan Books.

Elmore, R. F. (2000). *Building a new structure for school leadership*. Washington, DC: The Albert Shanker Institute.

Fullan, M. (1993). *Change forces: Probing the depths of educational reform*. London: Routledge.

Fullan, M. (2006). *Turnaround leadership*. San Francisco: Jossey-Bass.

Grossman, P., Wineburg, S., & Woolworth, S. (2001, December). Toward a theory of teacher community. *Teachers College Record, 103*(6), 942–1012.

Hurston, Z. N. (1937). *Their eyes were watching god*. Philadelphia: J.B. Lippincott Company.

Little, J. W. (1990, Summer). The persistence of privacy: Autonomy and initiative in teachers' professional relations. *Teachers College Record, 9*(4), 509–536.

McDonald, J. P. (1989, November). When outsiders try to change schools from the inside. *Phi Delta Kappan, 61*(3), 206–212.

McDonald, J. P., Mohr, N., Dichter, A., & McDonald, E. C. (2007). *The power of protocols: An educator's guide to better practice, second edition*. New York: Teachers College Press.

Neufeld, B., & Roper, D. (2003). *Coaching: A strategy for developing instructional capacity*. Providence, RI: Annenberg Institute for School Reform.

Poglinco, S., Bach, A., Hovde, K., Rosenblum, S., Saunders, M., & Supovitz, J. (2003). *The heart of the matter: The coaching model in America's choice schools*. Philadelphia: The Consortium for Policy Research in Education, University of Pennsylvania.

Rodgers, A., & Rodgers, E. M. (2007). *The effective literacy coach: Using inquiry to support teaching and learning*. New York: Teachers College Press.

Schön, D. A. (1987). *Educating the reflective practitioner*. San Francisco: Jossey-Bass.

Sebring, P. B., Allensworth, E., Bryk, A.S., Easton, J.Q., & Luppescu, S. (2006). *The essential supports for school improvement*. Chicago: Consortium on Chicago School Research at the University of Chicago. Retrieved November 1, 2007, http://ccsr.uchicago.edu/publications/EssentialSupports.pdf

Sizer, T. R. (1984). *Horace's compromise: The dilemma of the American high school*. Boston: Houghton Mifflin.

Spillane, J. P., Halverson, R., & Diamond, J. B. (2001, April). Investigating school leadership practice: A distributed perspective. *Educational Researcher, 30*(3), 23–28.

Stevens, W. D., with Kahne, J. (2006). *Professional communities and instructional improvement practices: A study of small high schools in Chicago*. Chicago: Consortium on Chicago School Research, University of Chicago.

Tyack, D., & Cuban, L. (1997). *Tinkering towards utopia: A century of public school reform*. Cambridge: Harvard University Press.

West, L., & Staub, F. (2003). *Content focused coaching: Transforming mathematics lessons*. Portsmouth, NH: Heinemann.

About the Authors

David Allen teaches secondary English education at the College of Staten Island. He has been a researcher at the National Center for Restructuring Education, Schools, and Teaching (NCREST) at Teachers College, Columbia University, Project Zero at the Harvard Graduate School of Education, and the Coalition of Essential Schools (then at Brown University). His work has focused on authentic assessment, teachers' collaborative inquiry, school coaching, and small schools. He has taught English and ESL in middle school, high school, college, and adult education settings. He received a Fulbright grant to study school reform in Poland. His most recent books are *The Facilitator's Book of Questions: Tools for Looking at Student and Teacher Work* (with Tina Blythe, 2004) and *Looking Together at Student Work, Second Edition* (with Tina Blythe and Barbara Powell, 2007).

Suzanne Wichterle (Suzy) Ort began her career as a social studies teacher at University Heights High School, an alternative school in the Bronx, and then as a teacher of English as a second language in the Czech Republic. She has worked as a research associate at NCREST on several research and development projects, including revamping the Regents assessment system in New York State and large scale studies of policy implementation in New York Community School Districts 2 and 3 (with the Center for the Study of Teaching and Policy at the University of Washington). She was a coach at Park East High School for the Institute for Student Achievement (ISA) from 2002–2007. She holds a doctorate in curriculum and teaching from Teachers College, Columbia University, and a master's degree in administration, planning and social policy from the Harvard Graduate School of Education. Currently, Suzy is an assistant principal at Park East High School in New York City.

Alexis Constantini graduated from Fordham University in 2001 with a bachelor's degree in biological sciences. In 2004 she got her master's degree in secondary science with a focus in biological sciences from City

College while a member of the New York City Teaching Fellows. She has been teaching at Park East High School since 2002.

Jennie Reist moved from Lancaster, Pennsylvania, to New York City after graduating from Penn State University. She began teaching social studies at Park East High School in 2005, and taught there for the next two years. She is currently taking a break from teaching to pursue other interests, such as a Guatemalan immersion program in the Spanish language. Jennie anticipates a return to teaching, while seeking her master's degree in education.

Joseph Schmidt graduated from Rutgers University in 1999 with a bachelor's degree in history. He received his master's degree in secondary education in social studies from Brooklyn College in 2006 while a member of the New York City Teaching Fellows. He has been teaching at Park East High School since 2001. Before starting in the New York City Public Schools, Joe taught for a year at Brooklyn Friends School.